KAWARTHA LAKES
STORIES

An anthology

KAWARTHA LAKES STORIES

Copyrights belong to the authors © 2016

Copy Editing by Arran McNicol at Editing 720

Contents

Introduction

Although the city of Kawartha Lakes is a rural area known for cottaging, fishing, and ice cream, it is much more than that. With this anthology I wanted to reveal other aspects of the area, to give local writers and readers a chance to show the city and its people the stories that go untold, the aspects of humanity that are often overlooked in our day-to-day experiences. I wanted to see Kawartha Lakes reimagined, viewed through the lenses of an array of genres.

Many of the stories show the darker side of Kawartha Lakes, aspects of ourselves that we might be reluctant to admit, including how we treat our elders, as you'll see in "Rough Justice" and "Beans." But the stories are not without humour, as shown most prominently in "A Prom To Remember," "The Shaman's Prophecy," and "Beans." Even the cottager experience is reflected in "Sturgeon Lake Memories" and "The Shaman's Prophecy." Kawartha Lakes is not without its ghost stories, so included here are tales incorporating hauntings as well. Some stories reveal the reasons people come to Kawartha Lakes, whether it's to escape as in "Unreasonable," or for solace, as in "The Night Duet," while others explore reasons to stay.

I'm very excited to bring you this collection. There are some amazingly talented writers in this area, and I can't wait to share them with you. While the stories you are about to experience come in all flavours, I think you'll find they carry a common theme of "home." With that in mind, it is my pleasure to welcome you to our versions of the city of Kawartha Lakes. Like the characters in the stories contained within these pages, may you fall in love and never want to leave.

STURGEON LAKE MEMORIES

Jean Booker

JULIE SAT ON the dock watching the sun-dappled waves lapping on the shore of Sturgeon Lake. It was almost ten years since she'd sat in this same spot enjoying the wonder of a weekend at Gran's cottage.

She'd always meant to come back to visit Gran, but time had slipped by. For the first five years after she'd moved out west she'd been busy with university, and after that her job with Canadian Tire. *How many times*, she wondered, *did I promise Gran I'd come and spend time with her at the lake?* Where she'd spent the first fourteen summers of her life. But then she'd met Bryan and there had been no thought of spending holidays with anyone but him.

"I will come soon, I promise," Julie had said to Gran the last time they'd spoken on the phone.

"Don't leave it too long, dear; I wouldn't want you to forget how special the lake is, and I'm not getting any younger, you know," Gran had urged.

Julie hadn't forgotten, but she had left it too late. Gran had died two weeks later, and now Julie had to keep her promise to visit the lake because Gran had left the cottage to her.

SHOULD I SELL the place? Julie wondered. She hated the idea of selling but didn't know what else to do. The place was old. She'd noticed that the faded white paint was peeling in places and one of the bedroom windows was cracked. She'd toyed with the idea of asking for a transfer to the Toronto office of Canadian Tire, but it would be a big move. A new job, no friends, sad memories of her parents being killed in a car crash when they were on a trip to Ontario—no Gran to visit—she wasn't sure she could do it. No, she'd have to sell the place.

Memories of perfect summers came flooding back—sun-filled days spent swimming and canoeing with kids from the other cottages; sing-alongs around roaring bonfires at night. And sailing—she smiled, remembering how excited she'd been when her dad had bought the sailboat, then how angry she'd been with herself when she'd kept flipping the stupid boat over. And that horrid red-haired boy who'd been visiting his aunt and uncle at the cottage next door. He'd kept following her in his canoe and laughing every time she tipped the sailboat. What was his name? She couldn't remember—Craig something or other.

The next summer her family had moved to Vancouver, taking the sailboat with them. Her parents had joined a sailing club and it was there, a couple of years later, she'd met Bryan. From then on her life had revolved around Bryan and sailing. Their breakup this past Christmas hadn't been easy, and Julie hadn't had the heart to date anyone since. She'd also vowed never to set foot on a sailboat again.

She decided to see what was in the boathouse before phoning the real estate agent in Lindsay. It was full of tools and several cobweb-covered Muskoka chairs. She remembered painting the chairs one summer as a surprise for Gran. Gran had been delighted but then had forgotten that the chairs were wet and got white paint all over her navy pants. Julie had felt awful about it, but Gran had just laughed and said she was starting a new fashion—polka-dot slacks. Dear Gran—how Julie missed her. *Not much of value here,* Julie thought as she looked around the boathouse. Then she saw the old green canoe. The paint was peeling, but apart from that it looked fairly seaworthy.

Should I? she asked herself. *Why not, just for old times' sake.*

She found a paddle, dragged the canoe out, and set off across the choppy water. The lake was deserted except for a lone sailboat out in the centre. As the paddle sliced through the water she realized her cheeks were wet—she was crying, crying for Gran and for not coming back sooner, and crying for herself because she couldn't bring back the past. She was in the middle of the lake when she saw storm clouds scudding across the sky. . .

She remembered storms could blow up quite suddenly on Sturgeon Lake, and turned to head back to shore. Waves began splashing against the side of the canoe and she heard thunder in the distance. Then heavy rain came pelting down from the sky and she wasn't making much headway as she turned and tried to paddle back toward the shore. It was then that she noticed the sailboat—and the man on board who was struggling to keep it under control. A gust of wind caught the sail and the boat suddenly capsized, sending him flying into the angry water.

He'll have trouble righting her in this wind, Julie thought. Then she saw that he seemed to be entangled in the mainsheet. She turned her canoe and paddled furiously toward the sailboat.

"KEEP STILL, TREAD water," she shouted as she steered her canoe alongside the floundering man and reached down to untangle him from the rope. Then the wind suddenly caught the sailboat and he was dragged away from her. Julie leaned further out and suddenly the canoe tipped and she was thrown headfirst in to the water. As she came up, the man managed to free himself, and struggled toward her.

"Are you all right?" he shouted above the noise of the wind.

"Yes—the boat—can we right it?" she yelled back. She watched her canoe being blown away as she swam toward the sailboat. It wasn't easy, but between them they managed to right the boat and climb aboard. Julie took the rudder as the man reached for the flapping sail and they battled their way back to shore and beached the boat.

"Come on," he said, taking her hand and running with her through the pelting rain. She realized he was pulling her toward the cottage next to Gran's. He flung open the door then struggled to close it against the wind. Curiously she looked around. She remembered visiting here. It hadn't changed much. Someone had put in a fireplace and some new chairs and a chesterfield, but the rest was basically the same as she remembered. The man disappeared into one of the bedrooms and returned with several towels and a fluffy white bathrobe.

"The bathroom's over there," he said, handing them to her.

"Yes, I remember," Julie said.

He gave her a strange look. "You remember?"

"Yes, I've been here lots of times—when I was a little girl. My Gran owns—owned—the cottage next door."

"Oh, you must be Julie. Your gran always hoped you'd come back. I was so sorry to hear about her death. She was a lovely lady."

Julie went into the bathroom, changed into the dry robe, and came out towelling her wet hair. He'd changed into jeans and a sweater and had started a fire in the living room. Outside, the rain was easing off and the wind had died down.

"I really appreciate your help out there. I shouldn't have gone out. I'm not that good with a sailboat. Lucky for me your sailing seems to have improved over the years."

"Improved?"

"Well, I remember one summer I was visiting my aunt and uncle, and I think you were just learning to sail and you kept tipping the boat. I was sure you'd give up, but I guess you didn't." He laughed as he rubbed his hair with a towel.

Julie noticed he was tall and good looking and there was something familiar about his smile. Then she noticed that his hair, which she'd taken for dark brown when wet, was actually a coppery red.

"You're not that horrid red-haired kid who. . ." Embarrassed, she stopped, but he was laughing again.

"I'm Craig Anderson. I bought the cottage from my aunt and uncle a few years ago. I guess your grandmother never mentioned it."

No, Gran never mentioned it, Julie thought. *But I have a funny feeling that's one of the reasons she was so keen to get me back to Sturgeon Lake. Gran never did like Bryan, although she only met him that once at Mom and Dad's funeral. She said I was wasting my time with him. But perhaps it wasn't a waste after all. If Bryan hadn't taught me to sail so well I wouldn't have been able to help Craig out there on the lake.*

"You live out west, don't you? How come you're here?" he asked.

"Gran left the cottage to me so I thought I'd come and take another look at it. I'd forgotten how beautiful it is here—when it's not storming, that is."

"If you're going to be around for a while, perhaps you could give me some sailing lessons," Craig said.

"I'm not sure what I'm going to do," Julie said. "I was thinking of selling the place, but I don't think I can. It holds too many memories."

"I think your gran would have liked you to keep it," Craig said.

Julie looked out at the now calm water of Sturgeon Lake. Canada geese were swimming just off shore and the sky was clearing. Puffy white clouds were taking over and suddenly a rainbow arced across the sky. *Maybe that was Gran sending me a message,* Julie thought, and she smiled as she turned to Craig and said, "I know she would, and who knows—maybe I will keep the cottage after all."

***

Jean Booker is the author of three novels, *Mystery House, Keeping Secrets,* and *Still at War*, and several short stories in newspapers and literary magazines. She lives in Bobcaygeon and is a member of CANSCAIP and the Writers' Union.

A Prom To Remember

Clint Cummings

TODD WAS SITTING on the edge of the Scugog River, feeling sorry for himself, when he heard a playful giggle nearby. Down the boardwalk, by the parking lot, a girl about his age said goodbye over her shoulder to a group of her friends.

Time stood still, as tends to happen in these moments.

Todd traced every movement of auburn hair as she turned toward him. He saw the tiniest bit of her tongue move across her mouth before she gave him a welcoming smile. Déjà vu set in as his heart raced.

Before she could speak, Todd blurted, "Will you go to the prom with me?"

Time stretched out, playing a cruel game.

Todd was acutely aware that the beautiful girl was standing above him, looking down. He turned his attention back to the black waters of the Scugog.

Why had he said that? Was it one last gasp before oblivion?

"I'm Teva," the girl said. "That was brave. Let's see how brave you really are. Talk to me."

She offered her hand and Todd helped her sit.

Unfortunately, Todd must have pulled her down too hard.

Teva stumbled. In a manic effort to keep her from getting a premature cleansing, Todd wrapped his arms around her and they ended up falling together in a clumsy lump on the boardwalk.

Teva got up abruptly, straightening her ruffled clothes.

"A little soon to go for a tumble together, I think." Teva offered her hand to pull Todd's red-faced form up.

"Thanks," Todd said.

Just when Todd thought he had blown his opportunity with this vision, she said, "Let's walk. It's a nice night for a walk."

Todd's heart did a flip while his shock and embarrassment

poofed away magically. He imagined chimes in the air at that thought.

Looking down at her clothes and with a slight shrug, she added, "Laundry day is tomorrow."

Teva studied him for a moment.

He said, "Okay," then "Sure!" more enthusiastically. He felt he had just missed something, though.

What he didn't miss was the red at the corner of her mouth as she grinned at his reaction. Should he tell her that her lipstick was smudged?

He decided to keep it to himself. It was only a little smudge.

Shara had really done a number on him by dumping him so close to prom. Todd did not want to ruin any chance he had with Teva and not being alone. The Scugog's call was too great.

They strolled to Bond Street and back to the locks. Though it was not that far a distance, somehow, the two of them stretched it and made their own pocket in time.

They talked and eventually he told Teva about Shara and how she had left him dateless for the last Big Night of his teen years. He told her how it had felt like his heart had been torn out.

Teva eyed him curiously. "That can happen."

While he pondered that response, her tongue darted out and the forgotten smudge disappeared. Pink erasing red. He almost felt the tiny shudder that seemed to ripple across her.

He gave his head a shake.

Todd was about to ask Teva about herself when she gave him another smile before saying, "I'll go to the prom with you. I'll be wearing white. Pick me up at the Old Mill Park playground."

She sprang up, breaking the spell. He was left in shock but with a great view of her tight jeans as she left him there.

PROM NIGHT ARRIVED both too soon and too slowly. Todd
had been longing for the night but feared that it would end badly
and the magic would be gone.

Todd waited at the playground in a basic black tux complete
with a fancy white shirt and bow tie. He had seen some guy in a
meme he had been forwarded wear one just like it. Shara had
said he would look handsome in it.

Todd's raven hair was long, and he felt it was a match for any
model's. He knew he looked good, but the bandage on his wrist
kept peeking out from beneath his sleeve, ruining the effect. For
such a small scrape, it just would not stop seeping blood, so
there was no choice.

When Teva appeared before him, he knew he looked just
right.

She was radiant in the fading sun. Her dress was white, as
promised, with beads and sequins sparkling and a small train
touching the earth. She looked like a modest bride rather than a
pending graduate. She wore the exact complement to his formal
attire. Had he told her what he and Shara had planned to wear?

"You are gorgeous," he stated as he presented and then
pinned a red corsage to her breast.

Teva laughed, looked him up and down, presented her arm,
and said, "Sweep me away, my dark prince."

Todd took her arm in his, guiding her toward his freshly
cleaned and polished pickup. The sun reflected off the metal the
way he hoped that the moon would that night. He had some
plans for this night that did not include a quick drive home
when the gym lights turned on. He had already dropped off his
grandfather's rowboat at the launch just up from where he had
met Teva. He hoped she would find it romantic when the time

came.

The evening progressed smoothly and, to Todd's mind, perfectly. He barely registered that Shara's expected date was there solo.

All of his focus was on Teva.

Forgotten were the friends, classmates, and teachers that had been so much a part of his life the past few years. They were there, but distant somehow. This very public event became something uniquely intimate between Todd and Teva.

The DJ announced the final song. Todd was still unsure of how to keep her from going home as soon as the last song was over. Time was short. This song was not a classic eight minute affair. He was stuck with a three-minute or less pop ticker to find a solution. Teva's small hand on his chest was both motivation and distraction. Her comfortable warmth stoked the fires within him. How on earth could he convince her to not go home right away?

The lights came on like a slap to the face.

Teva jumped away, just as startled as he was. She looked about her, somewhat flustered, and then refocused on Todd. Leaning forward slightly, Teva said in a slight Austrian accent, "I'll be back." She was off to the bathroom, with Todd left in her wake. Something tore away inside him.

Todd's confused "Okay" was left unheard in the air.

In a flash and without a sound, Teva was back. Her arm slid into his, pulling him to the doors.

"Come on. Let's go."

Todd did not like the sound of that. Had he blown it? How could he fix it?

When they reached the steps, Todd reached down to pick up the gown's train so that Teva would not trip. The train was not there. Teva had changed into a more casual black skirt.

He was looking at Roman sandals and bare legs. His hand froze in the air as he noticed her pink blouse. Where did her gown go?

Teva smiled down at him.

"Todd, what are you doing there?"

"Uhhhh. . ." Todd blushed and forgot the question he was about to ask.

Teva laughed at his discomfort and grabbed his hand to pull him upright.

"Let's go, big boy."

The pickup reflected the moonlight exactly as he had hoped it would. The truck practically glowed. Seeing that this part was going to plan, his confidence returned.

"Teva, I brought my grandfather's boat out. Would you like to go for a row?"

Teva stood on her tiptoes to give him a quick peck on the cheek, making his stomach flip, and said, "Of course I would."

Before he could move or react, she was on the other side of the pickup, opening the door and climbing into the passenger seat of the cab.

She's fast.

"WHAT A LOVELY night, Todd," Teva said from her perch on the tailgate.

Todd tossed his shoes and socks into the boat. The cool water splashed across his bare calves as he pulled the boat out of the reeds. "I'm glad, Teva. I had hoped for it . . . for us."

He brought the boat closer to the launch and the pickup.

With her legs swaying back and forth with a hypnotist's flare, Teva said, "Can you take my sandals off for me? I don't want to fall over."

The laces beckoned his fingers to the task.

As Todd knelt and grasped Teva's calf, he became aware of just how much shorter Teva's black skirt was in comparison to her white gown. His fingers tingled as they touched her exposed skin. His gaze drifted upward, trying to see beyond her knees. He was not always successful, but he was pretty sure that he had caught a glimpse of . . . something . . . up her thighs for his efforts.

Teva leaned back on her elbows, arching slightly, and did not seem to notice his wandering attention. He refocused on the laces.

"Are you done down there?"

Todd flushed. She had a way of keeping him off balance, that was for sure. One sandal came off. He placed it on the tailgate. As he fumbled with the next, he wondered how on earth she could have gotten into these things on her own, let alone so quickly at the dance.

When he finally slid the last sandal off her leg, he could not stop his fingers from lingering a little longer than necessary on her ankles before he released her calf to gravity.

"Done."

Teva jumped down into the water, swinging her legs up and over the gunnel into the boat. His vision sharpened and he caught how the shiny droplets trailed off her flesh back into the water. Before he could say something corny, he pushed the boat out and climbed inside.

As he started to pull back on the oars, Teva gazed at him. Her eyes flitted to the reddened Band-Aid and away. Todd pretended not to notice.

She said, "Let's float for a bit."

Relieved, Todd obeyed, letting the oars rest back in their locks. He would just use them to steer for now.

He studied the mysterious girl before him. She did the same with him. Their gazes held each other . . . not fast but still tight.

They did not speak.

They floated. They enjoyed their nearness, their proximity.

He briefly wondered if anyone could see them floating in the moonlight. He realized he did not care what anyone else saw or heard, not even when the first button of Teva's blouse came undone.

Todd's eyes widened and his grip on the oars tightened just a little more than when they had begun their innocent cruise by moonlight. He had hoped there could be some romance on the waterway tonight, but this promised to be more than he had dreamed. He did not believe anything, especially what he suspected was about to happen, would occur in a rowboat in the middle of town.

There must be something in the night air.

Todd let his smile take on what he hoped was a roguish air after her second button escaped from its trap. Revealed before him was a precious morsel of soft, beautiful flesh.

Teva's eyes twinkled as she moved her fingers languidly around and down to the next barrier. Todd made a motion to release the oars so he could help the process along, but Teva's hungry eyes made him stop for fear of breaking the spell.

"Row," she breathed. Another precious prize was exposed to the evening breeze.

Todd's mouth watered. His heart began to thud in an erratic beat. His ribcage felt like it was not even a minor hindrance. Only the buttons of his own shirt seemed to hold it in. Not even the trappings of a steady rhythm could contain the rising of his heart. His blood felt like it was squirting through his body rather than flowing smoothly. It was so unreal.

Everything floated away as they drifted beneath the Wellington Street bridge. All of Todd's senses were refocused on his prom date.

Todd kept his hands on the oars but leaned closer to Teva. His nails dug into the wood as he moved his mouth closer to hers. The fear that she would stop him rose, but he had to taste her. He needed to touch her lips. Now.

Teva moved her hands aside and welcomed his lips to hers.

The kiss was everything he had hoped for and more. Teva's moist lips tasted of peaches with a tinge of iron. The scent of the outdoors seemed to come from her hair and fill his nostrils. The combination caused a gentle sigh to escape his throat. He was pleased to hear it echoed from Teva, as well.

Surprisingly, there was no giving in to animal passion. Todd felt at peace, and when Teva placed a hand on his chest for the second time that night and pushed him back slowly, there was no resistance, and she only had to use the slightest of touches. For that moment, that small intimacy was enough.

"Row."

Todd rowed.

Teva's gaze reacquired Todd's.

As mischief played across her face, Todd thought back to earlier in the night at the prom and how he had been surprised when she changed out of her gown before they left. He thought that she was just uncomfortable in the thing. Was it symbolic? Did Teva have her own plans for this night?

"I think I love you, Teva," Todd whispered. His husky whisper sounded more like a bear than a Casanova. Todd flushed with embarrassment.

"You just might," Teva said.

Another button was pressed through another eyelet.

More skin, more warm, naked flesh.

The calm that had come from meeting Teva's lips was beginning to erode. Todd could feel something primal rising within him.

There was something otherworldly to this moment, to this moonlit night, bringing back the memory of when they had first met down by the boardwalk just a week ago.

They passed under the Lindsay Street bridge.

Todd's mouth watered. He was transfixed as Teva's tease went on. His own private performance.

The first signs of her own need started to materialize. She began to shift on the bench. As her thighs slid minutely across the hard wood, her skirt began to shift and flatten, following its own ebb and flow. Exposing more flesh and then hiding it again. It was a separate show from the finger play going on above. It was subtle and small, but it made Todd feel a bit reassured that this might not be just some trick or Gotcha! moment. Teva wanted him as much as he wanted her.

Todd's body reacted to this realization. His clothes began to constrict around him. He ripped the bandage from his wrist to release some of the constraint. Teva twitched at that.

His blood pulsed through him as it had before with every strange, erratic beat of his heart.

Another button. More flesh.

His temples throbbed. Teva's eyes were locked on his.

Another button. Another secret exposed.

His tongue darted across his lips to remoisten them and then retreated back into the safety of his mouth with his teeth closed and clenched.

Teva reflected the same struggle back at him. There was a feral look in her eyes.

Another button was set free.

How many buttons were there, anyway?

Todd felt his body heat rise. The yearning for each other was becoming unbearable, but he still took no action. Their willpower was unearthly in its resolve.

Todd was amazed that he could stand this. How much longer could he hold on?

The boat thumped against the shore by the Old Mill, and just like that, the leash was lost.

The time for restraint was shattered in the past.

No more tender games.

With that thump, Todd exploded at Teva. Teva met him mid-pounce, knocking them into the water. Had it not been the moment that it was, they would have laughed.

Instead, they shredded each other's clothes and made the water boil.

Todd gave in to his primal instincts.

Beneath the moon, their lust took them onto the shore as they took each other.

Todd changed and saw that Teva was changing too.

With horror and excitement, Todd realized that Teva was what he was becoming. He looked at his now healed wrist as their bones stretched and cracked in a macabre symphony. Teva had done this to him when they had literally fallen for each other at their first meeting. That had not been lipstick on her mouth.

Their fangs grew.

Their fur filled in even as Todd's humanity fell away.

Their cries of passion became howls to the moon.

Teva's patience and power had awakened Todd.
The she-wolf now had her mate.
Lindsay would never be the same again.

***

Clint Cummings is a writer in Kawartha Lakes.

THE NIGHT DUET

Stefan Ellery

CLINK. SILVER SPARKLES rose into the air. *Clink.* Another, smaller; a dime. *Clink.* Brass joined with the silver, danced in front of his eyes, and then faded. A rush of sparks followed. More clinking. Colours melded. *Clink, clink, clink, clink.* Copper exploded; pennies unwanted. Doug didn't care about the value.

Doug played the last bars of the song, and the sound of coins being thrown into his cello case came to an end. Doug looked at his watch; he had time for another piece. He touched the strings with his bow and closed his eyes to the city. He blinded himself from the tall buildings looming above him, the lights washing down on the pavement and the traffic trundling by. He pulled the bow along the strings. Bach's prelude floated into the air, the sound reflected back to him from glass and steel. He opened his eyes; only the sound of his music entered his ears. The city streets were silent; no engine roared, no child cried; footfalls were cushioned by the music Doug played.

His heart filled the cello; the sound he created wrapped onlookers with comforting colours. Doug ended the piece. He began again and interrupted the audience's desire to clap with plucking and hammering of the strings. The music sped up and classical became jazz; colours bounced all around him, and sweat slid down his face and along his neck. His muscles began to ache with joy and he pushed himself on. A thud mixed into the jingle of coins, giving him the colours of rot, and his stomach began to ache. He stopped playing and looked into his case. A well-worn boot sat amongst the coins. A dark-haired man in black pants and a colourless shirt turned away.

Doug discarded the boot, took the coins and put them into a pouch, and packed his cello back into its case. Disappointed, his audience realized his street performance was at an end. Doug had another ten minutes left before he had to leave, but the pain in his stomach continued and there was no way he could perform at the moment.

This was the curse of his synesthesia, and while he could see colours free themselves with each sound, not all colours and sounds were enjoyable. Some even inflicted pain. Doug strapped the cello onto his back, ran to Dundas station, and hopped on the subway. He hoped that by the time he got to the stage the feeling in his stomach would subside. He needed to perform better than his peers. The conductor was assigning a new principal, and he was sure it would be him. After transferring to a street car and a short ride and walk, he found himself standing in front of the outdoor stage at Harbourfront. He'd made good time. The conductor was riffling through his music sheets under the open tent; no other performer had shown yet.

Doug unpacked his cello and bow, put the case away, and sat in his chair on the stage. He drew his bow across the strings. The sound eased his stomach and he felt he would be able to perform properly tonight. His second stroke faltered when he saw the man who dropped the boot in his case speaking to the conductor. The conductor glanced at Doug with pursed lips.

Doug heard footsteps on the stage and saw the other musicians taking their place. He covered his ears before they sat down; the scraping and creaking of the chairs had always given him pinpricks of pain with the colour of hot white streaks slicing across his eyes. When everyone settled down, he uncovered his ears and took a deep breath. The conductor stood on the podium and tapped his baton on the music stand, drawing everyone's attention.

A large audience gathered around the stage as the concert's performance time neared. Doug ignored the slow-moving waves hitting the harbour wall, the gull's greedy shouts for food, and the lights that adorned the masts of the boats sitting in the dark water of Lake Ontario. He pushed aside the smell of sweet candy apple and sausages grilling on a vendor's barbecue. The conductor raised his baton, signalling the beginning of the performance.

The conductor's baton stroked the air and the strings sent out long tendrils of colour; the cellos followed, wrapping the streams in the hues of fall. Doug's was richer—the colours of his music always showed up more prominently than any other musician's. He wondered what it would be like to play with another who could match him. The kettle drums exploded, sending fireworks into the air, and the winds pushed out serene waves of blue.

The concert ended and the audience dispersed, as did the musicians. Doug remained.

The conductor walked onto the stage and took a seat beside Doug. "Why are you still here?"

Doug shifted in his chair. "I just need to rest before I head home."

"That's not what I mean. Why are you in an ensemble playing classical music?"

"I love music—hearing, feeling, and seeing it. What better place is there than in a concert?" Doug smiled as he said it. He always knew why.

The conductor pulled out a cell phone from his shirt pocket. "Perhaps on the streets." He then turned the face of the phone to Doug. A video of his street performance before the concert played on it.

"I don't understand."

"If you play in a concert, then classical music is what you should be playing—nothing else. Not rock, blues, or jazz. I don't care how good you are; the other styles you play will one day affect your performance in a concert, you'll mess up, and I don't need this. I will not take the chance."

"I won't mess up. I don't hear the music the same way. I see it. It doesn't allow me to make mistakes."

The conductor sighed. "I know your condition, but I don't know it well enough to trust in it. You are the best cellist I have known. You were going to be the next principal—but now?" The conductor shook his head. "Now, I can't have you performing with us anymore." The conductor handed him an envelope. "This is your final pay in addition to the next performances you were contracted for."

Doug stared; shock filled his stomach with butterflies. He watched as the conductor stood up and walked away.

The conductor paused. "Take some time and consider the direction you want to take your art."

Doug covered his face with his hands. All he could hear were the receding footfalls of the conductor leaving the stage.

DOUG WOKE UP with a headache. The TV glowed. Loud sounds came from the action flick playing on the television. Food wrappers and empty soda bottles lay strewn across the floor, and dirty clothing was draped across the backrest of the couch. The stale smell of leftover mac and cheese wafted in from the kitchen. *Bang bang.* Jolts of red pain passed in front of Doug's eyes. He pulled off the sheet covering him and groaned as he sat up. *Kaboom.* He covered his ears; his eyes blurred as the explosion washed the apartment in red. Not able to find the remote, he struggled to reach the TV, the destructive noise holding him back. The movie faded to black and a toilet paper commercial with a jingle took its place. The apartment filled with soft, pale clouds of pink. Freed from pain, Doug rushed to press the off button.

Knock, knock, knock. Doug closed his eyes and rubbed his temple. *Knock, knock, knock.* He cursed at whoever stood behind the door. He had a doorbell that played soothing music. It was there so he wouldn't have to hear the irritating sound or harsh colours of knocking. He opened the door, and his mother walked in. She gave an assessing look at him and his apartment with a wrinkled nose, and disgust plastered her face.

Doug chewed on his lip. He wanted to hurry his mother out. "Ma, come back later. I'll have the apartment cleaned up by then."

She rolled her eyes. "You won't, and I want you out of here." His mother tossed a small object at him. Doug caught it.

He opened his hand and stared at a key. "What's this for?"

"A house I rent out in Lindsay. One that happens to be empty at the moment."

Doug's brow furrowed. "Why are you giving it to me?"

She placed a hand on his shoulder, her eyes gentle. "Doug, I heard what happened."

Doug pulled away, his body stiffening. "Who told you?"

"There are people who care about you. They have been trying to reach you."

There were calls that he didn't pick up. All musicians from the orchestra. He didn't want their sympathy. They still had their places in the ensemble.

"I'll be fine. I just have to sort things out."

His mother kicked an empty bottle of cola; it rolled underneath the couch, joining the other waste he hadn't picked up. "Here? Locked up in your apartment? Eating and drinking junk food? No, you need a change of space. Get some fresh air, find yourself."

"Mom."

His mother held up her hand and dangled his apartment keys in front of his face.

"Don't you have anything else to do than bug me?"

His mother smirked. "The pleasures of retirement. Now get packed up; there's a bus leaving in a couple hours."

THE BUS STOPPED in downtown Lindsay at the corner of Cambridge and Kent. He carried his cello on his back and held a large duffel bag that his mother had packed for him. He should have been firmer with his mother and not let her push him around. He was an adult in his thirties, and independent. He waited for the light to turn green before crossing.

There was not much traffic; a couple of cars drove by, followed by a kid skateboarding in the middle of the road. The smell of cigarettes entered his nostrils, causing him to cough. Youth not even high school age stood against a blank brick wall smoking. He hoped he was doing the right thing coming to this town. Boutique shops lined each side of the road; a Pizza Pizza sat next to a small movie theatre—they looked to be the only places open. In the distance he could see a Tim Hortons. His stomach growled. It was a couple minutes to ten.

Harleys lined up at the side of the road next to Tim Hortons; people in their fifties dressed in leather and jeans gathered around talking to each other. A couple were admiring an old black vintage car. A bell chimed, drawing his attention to a large pale green building with a steeple. Next to it stood a red brick building where a sign on the walkway promoted The Lindsay Gallery. Another sign showed that the building also housed a library. A glass-enclosed flame flickered in front of the building.

Doug decided not to go into Timmy's despite the non-threatening classical music playing outside. He wasn't sure about the owners of the bikes, so he decided to stay on the far side of the road and head north. Large trucks surrounded a park; pictures of chicken and ribs were painted on the sides. A fence enclosed a bunch of tables that sat under an open tent. There looked to be an event—events brought people. Doug considered coming back in the morning with his cello to gather some coin.

He took a deep breath and filled his lungs. The air was fresh. Too fresh—it reminded him of the world he had left, the congestion of people and cars, flashing lights and harsh noises, all reminders that he wasn't alone. Doug kicked a loose rock into someone's front yard. Here there were no reminders; the street he walked beside was empty of traffic. A cat stalked a rabbit sitting in a patch of flowers. A cricket rubbed its feet. A rhythmic sound from a tree frog filled the night with woody colours. The sounds that he heard now were unnatural to him.

Maybe he should listen to his mother and the conductor; he certainly needed to rethink his position in life. He doubted he'd be continuing to play in an orchestra, not when he wanted to play more than just classical music. He wondered if he could make it as a soloist—he did it on the streets, but not as a profession. It was doubtful he would ever fit in with a group of musicians. Coming to Lindsay might give him a way to explore his music.

Doug had to walk up to the northward of Lindsay. If he were in Toronto he'd just hop on a bus or street car. There was no place he couldn't go in Toronto by public transit. It didn't look like he'd have that advantage in Lindsay. Thirty minutes passed by before he arrived. He looked at the house from the edge of the driveway. There were no lights to guide him to the door of the bungalow, and no one waited to greet him. He felt alone.

THE FIRST THING he did once he entered the house was to open all the windows; the house smelled stuffy and needed a good airing out. He found the master bedroom and lay on the unclothed mattress that had been supplied for renters. The sound of a flute drifted in through the open windows, bringing in calming colours that caressed his body. He wondered who played the flute. He enjoyed the sound and would love to see the musician who played so well. Doug let the sound of the flute ease him into a peaceful slumber.

Morning light landed on Doug's face; he opened his eyes to a new day. Breakfast consisted of a single bagel he'd bought from a bakery in Toronto. When he finished, he grabbed his case and pulled out his cello. Doug slid his hand along the curves of the instrument, feeling the tenderness the crafter had put into it. His cello was more than an instrument to him. It was his soul mate, his partner. He had no need for the love of a woman, not when he had an instrument that could give him a sense of bliss.

He stroked the strings with his bow, bringing forth the rich baritones from the cello. The room lit up with the light of the music. He hugged the cello and enjoyed the vibrations of sound on his chest. Doug played the prelude of Bach's Cello Suite No. 1. He moved his body back and forth with the instrument. The music and motions became a dance in a ball. His instrument, a woman he twirled with skill. He closed his eyes and felt the sensuality that he created. Doug, absorbed into to the music, didn't hear the knocking on his door until it became heavy-handed and sliced through the colours that surrounded him. He opened the door to find an elderly man with a stern expression.

Doug swallowed his anger at being interrupted and tried to be polite. "Yes?"

The elderly man pressed his finger to Doug's chest. "Can you keep it down? I'm on the night shift and really don't want to hear any racket while I sleep."

Doug crossed his arms. "Cellos don't make a racket."

The man snarled. "Cello, drums, guitars—I don't care what you're playing. They all make noise, and noises keep me up. Go play somewhere else. Try the trail or an empty field."

"Yeah, sure." Doug slammed the door. He had never had any issues with anyone before, but his practice in Toronto occurred when no one was home, or when he could get to the stage early and play before rehearsal started. Irritated, he didn't feel the desire to continue playing. He could have argued with the man, but being new in town, he didn't want to cause any friction.

He headed back downtown and, as he'd surmised, there were people at the event. Even the roads were filled with pedestrians. Swirling colours from country music draped around the crowd as they sat eating their food. A band played under a pavilion; the music was raw, showing limited experience. Still, the sound they produced had soul and lifted Doug's spirits. He took himself away from the gathering to a street corner where he could play without interfering with the band. A crowd began to form as he pulled his cello out of its case. He began his familiar process and created colours with each stroke of the strings. People were enthralled and stayed for his full set. Tired, he ended his performance and packed up. A young man with a shaved head stood in front of him.

"You ever played in a group?"

Doug laughed. "Yeah, I have."

"Good—we need another in our band. Your cello would really

attract people to our gigs. The bars don't pay much, but if we pack the house we get a bonus."

Doug lifted the cello onto his back. "I'm not sure if you really would want someone like me."

"I know we would. Loved your performance." He handed Doug a card. "You can think it over. Call me if you want to join us. We have a gig next week at the York, and practice is in a couple of days."

"Thanks." Doug walked away and headed back to his temporary home. The thought of playing with people gave him a good feeling, but he wasn't sure if he was ready.

DOUG TOOK A short nap. When he woke he had the urge to play his cello. Not wanting to deal with the grumpy old man, he went to look for the trail. It didn't take him long to find it—all he had to do was walk out into the backyard; he could see it on the other side of the chain-link fence. Beside the trail, an abandoned farmer's field lay fallow. Near the edge of the field Doug could see the frame of a swing set. No houses were near it. Further away, across the river, was a large building with lights surrounding it. It didn't look much like a factory—it could be the jail; he had no desire to find out. Doug thought it would be a perfect spot for him to practice.

He returned inside, grabbed his cello, and headed to the park. Daylight was fading, and he meant to make use of the solitude. He sat on a bench that faced the swings, and began the slow movement of the Swan from the Carnival of Animals, written by Camille Saint-Saëns. It felt like magic. The sadness of the music was accompanied by the setting of the sun. He played his cello like a lover running a finger down a woman's back, bringing pleasure with the softness of his touch.

A delicate breeze rose from the distance, accompanied by the floating sound of a flute. Its voice bound itself to the music of the cello, blending in with harmony. Doug played over and over again, the distant flute matching the brightness of the colours he produced. When he stopped the music, the sound of the flute faded away. Doug's breaths were heavy, and sweat drenched his body. He'd never been so moved as he was now, and for the first time in his life, he thought he might be in love. He had found someone who could match the colours of his playing. Doug was awed by the splendour that they created together, and wanted more. He began to play his cello again; he stopped after fifteen minutes, when the flute player didn't join him, and he gave in to his exhaustion.

The next evening he went back to the park. Doug didn't bring his instrument. He needed to seek out the source of the player who had spun a magical duet with him the previous night. Carrying the cello would bog him down.

The flute began with a cadence of slow, soft notes, tying his heart with its beauty. A thin strand of colour reached out to him, and he followed the changes of the notes toward the source. He came to a tall pillar that once supported a railway bridge, and perched at the top was a lithe woman playing the flute. She was covered by darkness, and he could only make out her shape, the stars above crowning her head like a queen. He wanted to climb the pillar and see her and her graceful movements. Doug needed to know who this woman was that could play the flute with elegance and heartfelt emotion. He touched the pillar and felt the sound with his hands. He saw the colours of intricate beauty and heard the splendour. Drawn like a sailor following the voice of a siren, Doug climbed the pillar. The music stopped, and when he reached the top, he found emptiness.

He looked down but could see no sign of her. He didn't know how she'd disappeared from his presence . . . he should have been able to see her from his vantage. Giving up, Doug climbed back down and headed home, disappointed that he didn't get to meet her.

Doug lay on the unfurnished living room floor. He wanted to know more about the woman. He wanted to hear the sound that made him fall in love, and he wanted to be her partner forever. Doug no longer had an interest in going back to Toronto. He was focused on another dream. He didn't care to be a soloist anymore. If he could be with the woman he saw, he could find happiness in performing duets with her. He had never felt his music join with another so intensely. Doug's eyes fluttered with the heaviness of sleep, and he fell into the richness of his dreams. The sound of a flute playing entered the house and surrounded his body with its sweetness.

Doug was well rested. He hadn't had such a good sleep in a very long time. Perhaps the country air agreed with him. Doug spent the rest of the day gathering supplies so he could make it through the week without starving.

That evening, he left earlier for the park to allow him more time to play his cello. He played for an hour and became restless without the presence of the mysterious woman. He needed to hear the flute again and caress her with his cello's music. Doug wanted to be held by the notes she played and feel the warmth contained within.

He only heard her playing once darkness fell onto the land. He decided he was going to get a closer look at the mysterious flute player. He walked to the pillar with cello in hand. She wasn't there. Afraid his presence might spook her, he hid behind the foliage of some wild sumac trees. He waited until the sun fell and the stars and the moon covered the night sky.

The music came again, a lullaby to soothe a baby and make its tears disappear. Spheres of colours surrounded the pillar, spreading outward and then disappearing as the notes faded away. He heard the music and saw the rainbow it produced, but there was no woman that he could see, just the sound. He stayed until the dawn broke and silenced the flute. He left with hope and regret and headed back home to get some rest.

The stars were out before Doug left the house with the cello strapped to his back; he had slept the whole day away. He didn't understand why he was so tired. Sure, he'd stayed up the whole night, but half a day would have sufficed. He hoped he was not too late to hear the melody that she performed. He ran out of the house and stared across the trail from his backyard, where he heard the enchanting flute playing. Doug sighed in relief. She was out there waiting for him to hear her music. He had the urge to pull out his cello, but believed if he did so, he would never get the chance to meet the woman who played so beautifully.

This time the colours were dim and the sound empty. It spoke of a loss and lonesomeness, of good times passed by. It was not classical music, but sounded more ancient, more tribal. He could feel and see the gaps in the sound, and Doug wanted to fill it in with his music. He felt for her, and could feel all the hurts she played. He hurried to the pillar and thought he saw the woman playing on top. He climbed the pillar but the woman wasn't there. Her music kept on playing so he looked all around on the ground, and then he saw her.

The moon lit her dark hair and pale face. She wore a red dress that flowed in the wind. Though her feet were bare, she was a picture of elegance, and exuded a Fae-like presence. She was as beautiful as the music she played. Doug filled in the gaps

of her music with the warmness of the cello. Playing on top of
the pillar gave him a surreal feeling; he knew his music would
reach out beyond the trail and enter nearby homes. He didn't
care, not when he felt the joy of filling in the loneliness the
woman expressed through her music. Her flute playing became
more solid; the music brightened and surrounded the night. If
people could see what he saw because of his synesthesia, they
would think they were looking at the Northern Lights.

Doug and the woman played for hours, wrapping each other
in their composition. He let her play alone, and she picked up
the pace, bringing high notes of laughter and cheer. He sat on
top of the pillar, wishing to be closer to her. The howling of the
coyotes and a lone song of a loon blended into their music,
adding another dimension of beauty. He felt alive and enjoyed
the strange experience. Again with the rising of the sun, the
woman disappeared. He was disappointed, but still had the hope
he would get closer to her in the coming night.

Doug had set his phone to wake him before the light of the
day diminished. He didn't bother practising at the park. He
walked with purpose to the railway pillars, and once there, he
leaned on its surface and waited for the night. This time when
she showed, she was less than ten feet from him. She placed the
flute to her lips and tantalized him with sparkles of sound. He
moved closer toward her, but she backed away from him and
smiled with her eyes. Her music became richer, and she
distanced herself even more. Doug kept on following, led by her
music.

She didn't slow down for him to catch up. Instead she teased
him with the colours her flute playing made. He followed, blind
to everything but the vividness of her music. The ground became
rough, and he stumbled over his ankle. He didn't care. With the

weight of his cello strapped to his back, Doug raced toward her until the ground disappeared from him, and he fell into the river.

LESLEY HAD NO choice but to play his bagpipes in the park away from all the northward residences. His family never cared for the sound, and the neighbours wished he would disappear along with his pipes. Few appreciated the complexity and the harmony he could create with his instrument, except when he played in the fall parade. That was the rare time when people opened up their ears and allowed the music to enter their hearts.

The setting of the sun came all too soon, and he stopped playing. His pipes were loud, and he knew it would enter people's homes when they were trying to eat dinner, or sitting in their yards enjoying the warmth of a summer's night.

In the distance, he heard a flute and a cello playing together. It was a graceful love song, and Lesley was happy to stop practice and listen to their tune. Curiosity hit him, and he searched out the makers of such beauty. It took him a while—their music covered a large distance. He managed to make it to the railway pillars, where he looked up and saw the shadows of a woman and man. They were floating in the air. The hairs on his body rose. Whatever they were, he didn't want to take a closer look. He left them in peace, content to leave their music behind him.

***

Stefan Ellery is a multi-genre author who writes horror, YA paranormal, and children's stories. He has short fiction published in three different anthologies, a few self-published children stories, and two self-published novels.

THE SHAMAN'S PROPHECY

Vivienne Barker

SYLVIA AND SUSAN had been school friends in the East End of London, and had maintained their friendship from across the Atlantic Ocean, first with letters and the occasional phone call, but these days, much more conveniently, by email. They shared the trials and tribulations of their lives, and each time Susan suffered yet another miscarriage, Sylvia offered a "cyber" shoulder to cry on. But lately Sue spoke more about the gulf between Jim and herself—how happy they used to be, and how they didn't seem to have as much in common now.

When Sylvia offered the all-expenses-paid holiday in Toronto, Susan had accepted eagerly. Maybe it would help. God knew they hadn't had a holiday in years; every spare penny had been spent on the quest to have a child. Test after test, and then the last resort of in vitro, which had cost a fortune, and still no baby at the end of it. Yes, they needed a break if they were to salvage their marriage.

Jim agreed reluctantly. Sue's friends lived the high life, whereas he was a "pint at the pub with the lads" man, and one city was much like another—but Sue wanted to go, and a free holiday? He couldn't think of good reason to refuse. The tickets arrived, and a few weeks later they were on their way: their first trans-Atlantic flight, their first flight anywhere, in fact, and first class, too!

They'd no sooner unpacked their bags in Sylvia and Frank's luxurious condo when bad news arrived.

"Darlings, the most awful thing," Sylvia said. "We absolutely have to go to L.A. Something dire has happened at the office there, and we just have to go and sort it all out. Couldn't have come at a worst time, all my lovely plans for your holiday—well, of course you can stay here, and you only have to phone our office and they will get you tickets to anything you want to see, but I hate leaving you here to cope on your own."

At this point, Frank chimed in. "Of course, if they'd rather have a few days at the cottage . . ."

As the offer of their second home arose, Jim perked up. The way Frank described the place, it sounded wonderful: a lakeside cottage, fishing, use of their boat—that was more like it.

"It is rather remote and basic, but we keep it well stocked . . . It's a possibility?" enquired Sylvia doubtfully.

"We'd love it, wouldn't we, Susan? Where is it exactly?"

"In the Kawartha Lakes district. We'll have to give you a map; the GPS is a bit unreliable once you're off the main road. We'll have Giles take you in the limo, if you'd prefer."

"Oh, that's very kind, but I think we'd be happier hiring a car. That way we can see all the sights."

"If you insist, but there's not much to see; it's very rural," said Sylvia.

"Sounds wonderful. We'll leave right away and get out of your hair."

"You didn't have to sound quite so enthusiastic, Jim," whispered Susan as they made their way to begin packing. "I hope they didn't catch on that you're happy to leave."

"I'm sure they didn't. They've a lot on their minds, probably glad to be rid of us," he replied.

AFTER BIDDING THEIR hosts farewell, not too enthusiastically, Susan hoped, for they really had been kind, she and Jim set off in the hire car that had been delivered to the front door of the condo.

"Now that's what I call service," remarked Jim.

Susan clutched a printed road map and a handwritten sheet of paper with directions for once they were off the main roads.

After the bland drive along the 401 Highway, they turned north and the road started to wend its way through pine-shrouded hills and farmland. Cows of every breed studded the landscape, and nearly every property had a few horses in paddocks.

"This is more like it. Trees are trees and fields are fields, but somehow, you just know you're not in England. It's lovely countryside, but so—empty," said Jim.

The further north they went, the more the landscape changed, becoming rockier. The road had been blasted through the multi-hued rock shield, dropping down past sparkling lakes and petrified forests poking out of swamps. Herons occasionally flew upward in panic as the car disturbed their peaceful existence.

"Stop!"

Jim slammed on the brakes. "What?"

"That was our turnoff."

"God, you nearly gave me a heart attack. I'll back up; there's nothing coming," he said, looking in the rear mirror.

The map directed them up Fire Lane 45, which was little more than a cart track—rutted and narrow, with trees looming over and shrubs brushing the side of the car.

Some distance in, coming from an even narrower pathway, a young woman appeared on an all-terrain vehicle. Waving them down, she told them to follow her, introducing herself as Laureen, but no more information than that.

Taking off at a pace far faster than Jim would have liked, they followed along the winding track, and sometime later, they all arrived at a clearing where a lake sparkled through the trees beyond.

"Bloody hell," exclaimed Jim as he exited the car. "Are you

sure this is the right place, Susan? I thought we were coming to
a cottage in the woods, not a mansion in a jungle!"

"Jim, did you really expect Sylvia's cottage to be anything
else? You've seen her penthouse in Toronto! I know this is a bit
much, but she's given it to us for almost a week, completely free,
and if nothing else, I'm sure the wine fridge will be fully
stocked!" While Susan knew that Sylvia had done extremely well
after emigrating to Toronto, she was awestruck by the luxury in
which her friend now lived.

"You don't seem like Sylvia's normal sort," muttered Laureen
as she took off her black helmet, allowing her raven-black hair to
cascade over her shoulders.

"Oh, two heads, one eye . . . ?" Susan cut Jim off with a quick
jab to the ribs.

Laureen laughed. "Nah, more yer furs and diamonds set.
Dunno why they bother coming up; never set foot outside the
house except to arrive and leave. Still, it takes all sorts, don't it?"

"Um, who are you, exactly?" enquired Susan.

"I just help out occasionally. I'm your nearest neighbour, if
you like; twenty minutes on the ATV or two hours by road. My
number's on a pad in there, if you're stuck. Plenty of food in the
fridge and freezer. You know how to work a barbecue?"

Struggling to keep up with her rapid way of speaking, and
flitting from one subject to the next, Jim replied that he did
know how to light a barbecue.

"I'd better show you anyway, not like any barbecue I've ever
had." She led them to what appeared to be a professional
outdoor kitchen on a huge deck with a screened canopy.
"Screens go back if you want. Don't recommend it unless you
like black flies! Anyway, here it is."

The barbecue resembled a small crematorium. After showing

the two of them the intricacies of starting it, Laureen led them to a large fridge enclosed in a wall of cupboards.

"See, plenty to eat, but there's more inside. Make sure you lock the cupboards or raccoons'll get in." Beside the fridge stood another, this time full of wine.

"Look at this: I ain't never seen anything like it—special temps for red and white. We just keep our wine on a rope dunked in the lake. Not that we drink a lot of wine; beer's more our thing. You've got the code to get in the house? Same for the boathouse. Nice in there, same facilities but on a normal scale, if you know what I mean. I don't know anything about the boat. You'll have to figure that out for yourselves. Right, I'll be going. Don't bother with your cell phone—no reception. House phones work, but if you have an emergency, best get in the car and go. Police take forever to get here, and fire engines can't get up the track. House has got sprinklers, though!"

Reeling from the rapid-fire information and instructions, the two of them stood, mouths gaping, as Laureen drove away in a cloud of dust. Collecting their thoughts, they walked around to the front door.

"Ouch! Jesus, I'm bleeding. What the hell is with the mosquitos here?" Jim slapped at his face and arms.

"I think that's the black flies. I hope there's bug spray in here; I don't intend staying indoors," replied Susan, opening the magnificent pine front door.

After depositing their luggage, Jim left Susan to roam around the house.

"I'm going down to the boathouse. Can't wait to see if the *Queen Mary* is docked in there." He laughed.

"Jim, stop it. We can have a lovely time here. It's so peaceful and we've got it all to ourselves. Wait! I'll check the bathroom for bug spray."

But Jim was already out the door and on the path to the lake, slapping his face and arms as he went.

Roaming from room to room, Susan located a smaller bedroom and dropped their bags on the bed. The en suite bathroom was luxurious, and as she ran her fingers over the porcelain of the Jacuzzi bathtub, she closed her eyes, dreaming of the deep, sudsy bath she would take that evening. She wondered if perhaps she could persuade Jim to join her.

"Susan, Susan, where are you?"

Susan was brought out of her bubble reverie. "Coming," she called, and joined Jim in the pine-panelled living room. Floor to-ceiling windows were letting in the last of the day's sunlight, and suddenly she realized how hungry she was.

"The boathouse is great. Come and see it," Jim said excitedly.

"It's getting dark, and I'm starving. I'll see it tomorrow, but now I need to investigate the freezer and get some dinner on the table."

An hour later, Jim had mastered the barbecue, and an appetizing aroma was rising from two T-bone steaks found in the closet-sized kitchen freezer.

It wasn't long after eating that they were feeling the effects of the long drive and a full stomach.

"Think I'll turn in," said Susan sleepily.

"I'll just check the doors and I'll be there too. All this fresh air is making me tired too," replied Jim.

"JIM, I CAN'T sleep!" whispered Susan.

"You had enough wine to knock out a horse. What's the problem?"

"It's too quiet; there's not a sound."

"Not much we can do about that unless you want the stereo turned on."

"No," she replied sleepily. "I'm getting sleepy now."

"Good for you. I'm wide awake now," he replied grumpily, but was soon snoring gently.

A loon on the lake interrupted the perfect peace, but the two slept on, enjoying the breeze coming through the open window. Suddenly Susan awoke, sitting bolt upright, listening. Someone was trying to get in. She could hear doors being rattled.

"Jim, Jim, wake up! Someone's trying to break in!"

Jim yawned, reluctant to wake from such a deep sleep. "Don't be daft, woman. Who'd ever find this place?"

"I tell you, someone's out there. Get up and look."

"This place is like Fort Knox. Even if there is someone out there, they'll never get in."

"I don't care; get up!"

Jim arose and made his way to the living room. Peering groggily through the window, he was immediately wide awake when he made eye contact with a large bear, who appeared to be wrestling with the barbecue.

Uh-oh. The barbecue tipped over and crashed to the ground. A screaming Susan ran into the room and clutched him.

"How many are there? Is it a gang?" she whispered.

Jim was in a quandary. Would Susan be more upset at the thought of a bear or a gang of thieves on the premises?

"It's just an animal, nothing to worry about."

"What kind of animal, and what's it doing?" she asked timidly.

"We should have cleaned off the barbecue. It's just a bear, giving it a good licking." With more confidence that he felt, he joked, "No way will it get in here; Sylvia would never allow it."

The bear, having cleaned the barbecue thoroughly, gave it one last shove, then ambled down the path and into the bush. Sylvia and Jim made their way back to bed, sleep not returning easily, but toward dawn they were sleeping soundly.

RISING LATE FROM their disturbed night, Jim and Susan found the sun beaming and the day already warm.

"I'm going skinny-dipping," announced Jim. "You coming?"

"Jim, we can't. You go if you want, but I'm not."

She watched as he ran down the path, shedding his pyjamas as he went, reminding her of their carefree days when they were first married. Not that he'd ever run naked outside, but they were always laughing, doing silly things. Why had everything changed?

Jim rushed into the water, diving headlong. As he surfaced, the strangest sound escaped from his lips—a cross between a scream and a gurgle. He turned and yelled, "Christ, it's cold!"

Susan followed down the path, stopped, and doubled up with laughter as Jim came out almost as quickly as he had gone in, his body a few shades of blue in <u>all</u> the extremities.

Lying on the grass trying to warm his shivering body in the sunlight, he pulled Susan down beside him.

"I need warming up; skin to skin, or I'll die of hyperthermia." He laughed. "Come on, no one will see."

"Oh, Jim, you are awful." She giggled as his frozen fingers pulled the robe from her warm body.

The heat emitting from her soft skin ignited a long-forgotten passion, and having given in to their pent-up lust for each other, they finally broke free, lying side by side in the warm sun, panting, too exhausted to speak, amazed at what had happened.

That evening, they relaxed on the boathouse verandah,

watching the sun disappear in a glorious blaze of gold and pink.

"Let's stay here tonight," suggested Susan. "I like being near the lake, and maybe the sound of the water will help us sleep."

"I don't think that'll be a problem tonight, but okay. I'll get our stuff and we can sleep here. The bed's a bit small, but we can cuddle up, can't we?"

"I've had enough of your cuddling up for today!" Susan retorted primly.

Dusk was turning into darkness, the breeze rustling leaves, casting shadows. Susan standing, leaning on the railing, suddenly stiffened. She pointed at the mist rising from the lake.

"Jim, there's someone down there. Look."

Thinking it was the bear again, Jim suggested they move inside.

"It's not the bear," she said. "It's—it's— I don't know what it is, but it's coming closer."

The shaggy body stopped at the edge of the lake, light from the rising moon outlining its form. It turned and started moving toward them. It was a human with long hair and beard, dressed in animal skins and carrying a long stick.

Riveted to the spot, Jim shouted, hopefully with more authority than he felt, "Who are you? What do you want?"

The man spoke. "Do not be afraid. I am Kootna. I mean you no harm. You are not the inhabitants of this building." It was more a statement than a question.

"No, but we have permission to be here."

"Ah yes, permission from people who disrespect the land. But you are different. I bring you blessings."

"Thank you," replied Susan, wondering if she and Jim were seeing things.

"You have no children," stated Kootna.

"How did you know?"

"I know many things. There will be a child. The spirits see your sadness."

"That would be nice, but we're too old, and we had all kinds of tests." Susan sighed.

"No matter. The spirits have spoken. One was here last night."

"That was no 'spirit' on the deck last night. That was a bear. It attacked the barbecue. We saw it."

"Look." Kootna gestured toward the water, where the moonlight cast a silver glow over the mist, and sure enough, the shadow of a bear drifted across the lake. "Your life will be filled with a deeper purpose. Believe in the magic and healing that this purpose will bring."

The two of them watched the shadow as it moved across the water. Jim was first to regain his voice. Turning back to Kootna, he was about to ask how he did that, but Kootna had disappeared into the darkness.

"We're hallucinating, aren't we?"

"I don't think two people have the same hallucination," whispered Susan. "How incredible was that?"

"Humph. Lot of mumbo jumbo. We must have had too much wine. Let's go in; it's getting cold. I'll make sure all the doors and windows are locked!"

Jim may not have believed what he saw, but Susan carried Kootna's words into her heart. A child. Could Kootna make that come true? Certainly their lovemaking by the lake had more intensity than she had ever known before. Could it be possible?

The next morning, Susan was awake early, rising carefully so as not to wake Jim. She made her way to the big house. Climbing the steps to the deck, she walked across to the fallen barbecue and lifted the now buckled lid. It was clean, just as Jim had said it would be. That was certainly not a spirit, but the one by the lake . . .

Back at the boathouse, Jim had awoken, and, determined to make sense of what they had seen, or maybe just dreamed, walked along the shoreline, looking for any evidence of the old man's visit. No footprints marred the pristine sand. Jim shook his head. He could not explain the visions with any degree of satisfaction or sanity.

Thankfully the real bear never returned, but after each meal they were careful to clean off the barbecue, just in case. The old man, having delivered his message, didn't make another appearance, and none of the shadows on the lake resembled his companion again.

The rest of the week passed uneventfully, and all too soon it was time to leave. Bags packed into the car, Susan stood on the boathouse deck for the last time. Jim joined her, and, putting his arms around her, said gently, "Don't put too much stock in what we think we saw. I'd like to believe it, but it's not possible."

"I know, Jim, but it's been a good week for us, hasn't it? I know you've been as disappointed as me that we haven't been able to have a child, and I know that we have to put that wish aside, and get on with living. I've spent too much time wrapped up in misery and I've made you unhappy too. So from today, I want us to live our lives for us and be happy. It's not too late, is it?"

Jim brushed a tear away from Sue's cheek and held her close. "I never wanted anything else, you know."

ONCE AGAIN, THEY were back in the luxurious condo, and their hosts were anxious to hear if all had gone well.

"We had a wonderful time. There was so much to see and do," gushed Susan.

"Really? I find it just too dull, unless we've got people in, of course," replied Sylvia.

"Susan had a grand time at a step and fiddle contest," Jim said. "She got herself roped in to the step contest, and earned an honourable mention!"

"Yes, we went to country fairs, antique shops, and did you know there's an incredible lift lock in Peterborough? I've never seen anything like it," added Susan. "Oh, and the shaman."

"Shaman? What are you talking about?"

It suddenly occurred to Jim that the events of that night would sound totally absurd to this sophisticated couple.

"Just a man we met. He told us a lot of things," he said. "Your neighbour, Laureen, was helpful, though, getting us settled."

Susan opened her mouth to tell of Kootna's prophecy, but before she could, she felt a swift kick on her ankle. "Ow."

"Sorry, dear. I was just feeling around for my serviette; I dropped it. Help me find it, will you? I think it's near your foot," said Jim, giving his wife a very peculiar look.

The two of them bent down until their heads were below the table.

"Don't say anything about the shaman and the spirits. They'll think we're nuts!" Jim whispered.

"Ah, here it is," said Jim, waving his serviette as he sat up.

"As long as you had fun," replied Sylvia, looking sideways at her husband.

"Oh, and the black bear! Don't forget the bear," added Jim. "I'm afraid your barbecue is a bit battered."

"No! How awful for you. You must be glad to be going home

after such a fright," exclaimed Susan.

"No fear, we had the best time ever," Jim responded enthusiastically, looking at Susan.

Next morning, the limousine was waiting, and having said their goodbyes, Susan and Jim were whisked to the airport. Passing the long lines of people waiting to check in, Susan and Jim headed for the almost empty desk for first-class passengers.

"You know, Susan, I don't think I ever want to travel any other way," said Jim wistfully as they were shown to the lounge to await boarding.

"Don't get used to it. If we ever fly again, we'll be lining up with all the rest!"

Settled once again in the comfort of their first-class seats, Jim was looking rested and relaxed as he thumbed through the inflight magazine. Susan took a last look at Toronto out of the small window. Her mind drifted back to Kootna's words. She touched her stomach tentatively; could it be possible? She'd felt a little queasy this morning, but that could just be nerves about the flight. It was nonsense, all nonsense—wasn't it?

***

Vivienne Barker, born and raised in England, now resides in the beautiful Kawartha Lakes area of Ontario, Canada. Having worked for "the man" all her adult life, she decided to finally do what she wanted, which was looking after animals. Her company *Four on the Floor (and a Tail)* was a passion for five years prior to retirement.

Having retired, she started writing *The Train Now Leaving,* a semi-biographical historical novel which is slated for publication by Black Opal Books in the fall of 2016.

Excited to find the Kawartha Lakes Writers, she took up her "pen" again and began writing an eclectic number of short stories, "The Shaman's Prophecy" being one of them.

ROUGH JUSTICE

Tiffany Short

THE PUNGENT SMELL of regurgitated food fills my nostrils, making another round of throwing up a distinct possibility. My nerves have gotten the better of me, for the moment, at least. Feeling this sick won't deter me; there is no real plan for what I am about to do—I've just reached a point where nothing else makes sense. Here it comes; my throat is retching and gagging repeatedly as my body tries to expel any remaining stomach contents into the awaiting porcelain bowl. When I am able to, I reach for the toilet paper and tear off a strip so that I can wipe the filth from my mouth. Disgusting! I flush the contents down and step uneasily out of the stall.

The reflection in the mirror is unrecognizable. My skin is grey, but that could be my nerves. It lacks the deep brown colour that had been etched in from years of working in the sun. I maintain my tan these days by working in my late wife's garden. Salt and the lingering odour of vomit drift up to my nose. Cupping water in my hands, I slurp the cool liquid to remove the bitter taste from my mouth. My body shivers from the lingering cold sweat. Splashing water on my face, I continue to regain composure. I finger-comb my hair, trying to repair how disheveled it had become. The silver strands were wet and sticking to my forehead. Nerves would give me away. I begin to fidget, twisting my wedding ring around my finger several times. I whisper, in the otherwise empty bathroom, "Please forgive me."

The hustle and bustle in the mall carries me out of the washroom undetected. I am just another body in a mass of shoppers. I have to make my way to the bank. It is almost closing time; if I am going to follow through, I have to hurry.

The teller is fairly young. Her whole life is ahead of her. She still has hopes for her future. She smiles kindly at the elderly man I have become. I reconsider, but only for a moment.

The young woman accepts my bank book and types my account number into her computer.

"Hi, Mr. Griffiths. How are you today? Are you feeling all right? You look a little pale." She reaches across the counter to touch my hand.

"Uh, I'm f-f-fine, thank you." I move my hand away, not wanting her to feel how clammy it is.

She returns her hands to her keyboard, poised and ready. "What can I help you with?" I feel envious that she knows how to work the computer.

I slide a note across the table. I don't want a big scene. Her smile disappears and her eyes grow wide. Her hand, which continues to hold the note, is visibly shaking. I want to ease her discomfort. I'm not a bad guy. It has never been my intention to cause someone distress. She turns slightly and looks toward the end of the counter like she is going to walk away from her partition. Not wanting her to raise the alarm to the other workers, I catch her eye and whisper that she needn't go anywhere. I stammer slightly when I ask her to hand me the money she has with her. Her eyes are pleading. She is uncomfortable with my request and yet she isn't certain what consequences will follow if she doesn't take me seriously.

To be honest, I don't even really want to be here. I am supposed to be happily enjoying my retirement. I start twisting my ring around my finger, thoughts drifting to my former life. My wife and I had a farm outside of Little Britain, where we raised beef cattle and grew organic vegetables before retirement.

The teller quickly puts bills into an envelope, then slides it across the counter to me. The outside has a number scrawled across it to indicate how much she was able to collect from her

register. I nod, choke out a thank you, and shuffle to the exit.
The teller doesn't waste time; as soon as I reach the exit, she's at
the office of the bank manager. A quick glance back and I see the
young woman is shaking in front of her boss. I head out of the
mall, and it doesn't take me long to get into my old truck.

THE TRUCK STARTS just fine, due to my routine maintenance
schedule. I let out a big breath, trying to exhale my nerves, which
seem to have entangled with my respiratory system. Gripping
the wheel, I drive with greater caution than usual, mindful of my
speed, as I don't want to draw attention. I am sure that there will
be a warrant issued for my arrest just as soon as the facts are
reported to the police.

I need to get out of Lindsay. I drive down Kent Street,
turning left onto Lindsay Street then right onto Queen Street.
Heading out by Pigeon Lake Road, it seems more likely I can
remain hidden in the rural backroads. I switch on the radio to
91.9 Bob FM so I can keep tabs on any news about what I have
just done.

*"This is 91.9 Bob FM. We have clear skies this evening with a
chance of snow overnight. It is five thirty p.m.; be sure to listen
in for all the local news at six."*

The road bends and curves, my mind moving between past
and present. I need to figure out how to get the money to my
daughter. It rests in my jacket pocket by my heart. It had to be a
banking error, that such a large sum was removed from my
account, leaving me unable to help my daughter.

An error on their part, so I wasn't really robbing the bank—I
was trying to amend their mistake, something they were
unwilling to resolve. They set me up with internet banking in the
first place. I told them it wasn't any use, that I was too old for

something like that. They decided they were moving away from paper and pushed internet banking on me. Technology and seniors go together about as well as cats and water.

Headlights shine from around the curve ahead—looks like a police car. A quick check of my speed and I see that I need to ease off the gas. I check the rearview, but it's clear. As the car gets closer, my heart pumps faster and my hands begin to sweat. My breathing slows, perhaps to compensate for the jackrabbit in my chest. When I see that I am in no immediate danger of being caught, that the car doesn't belong to the OPP nor the Kawartha Lakes Police, just an average Joe, I let the air out of my lungs, gasping for fresh oxygen. I wipe my hands on my pants. My ring swivels on my slippery finger. With that I am lost in memory.

Grace and I thought we would move into town when we retired so we could save on expenses. The sale of the farm enabled us to just pay off our debt. We rented a small house in Lindsay; no need for a mortgage at our age and on our fixed income. At the time, we were blissfully unaware how important being close to the hospital and doctor's office would be in the years that followed.

Grace had started to experience respiratory issues. She thought it was asthma, a condition that was familiar to her; she had inhalers that were taken on an as-needed basis. She began to rely on them without much improvement. She went to her doctor and they recommended tests in order to properly diagnose. Lung cancer.

She went through chemotherapy and radiation. It was horrible to watch and not able to help in any real way. Cancer is an ugly battle. Last autumn, Grace's battle ended. That she is at rest and no longer suffering is my only consolation.

A tear slides down my cheek. I wipe my face roughly with my

hand. It's getting late. I no longer drive at night; so even though I want to get out of the area, it will have to wait. I have made it to the north end of Pigeon Lake Road, with the highway coming up shortly. Now that the adrenaline is easing out of my system, I'm going to crash.

I check out a cottage with a long driveway, hidden from the road by trees. Being November, cottage season is over, and the odds are in my favour that I can find a place to stay for the night. I drive up slowly. Everything is silent; I quietly leave my truck. With as much stealth as I can muster, I look into the windows. The rooms are dark and clean. The door is locked. I locate a hide-a-key under a flower pot. The key makes me feel better about entering the cottage.

The door opens to a mud room. I remove my boots out of habit more than anything. A sofa in the centre of the room faces a fireplace. Across from a recliner is the TV. The walls are a neutral shade, some beige-y, grey colour. The wedding photos catch my attention. They take me back to thoughts of my own wedding. Grace was gorgeous in her white gown, the prettiest bride to have ever walked down an aisle. Her father walked alongside her, beaming, knowing he was walking with an angel. The guests were our families, neighbours, and close friends. People who would never guess that I would rob a bank.

I find a package of crackers in the cupboards, and locate a glass. I turn on the faucet, but the water has been turned off for the winter. I look around some more and find a few bottles of water. I fill the glass and move to the couch. It has a blanket draped across the back of it, which I lift up and settle over my legs. The crackers are stale, but I can't be picky about snacks I have stolen. When there is nothing left but crumbs, I shuffle further down the couch and close my eyes.

I wake up around two needing to use the washroom. Where the hell am I? My heart begins to race. I sit up and rub my eyes. The urgency that woke me from a deep slumber makes me get up from the couch. The cottage is dark as I make my way to the bathroom. I quickly relieve my bladder and use one of the water bottles to wash my hands. Doubtful that I will fall asleep easily, I decide to investigate the cottage. A map will be helpful in planning my travel in the coming morning. I turn on a light. I look out the window and see that the snow they had been calling for has started to fall. The flakes look soft, and settle slowly onto the ground. The cottage seems to be well isolated, trees surrounding the grounds. I move across the room and check the drawers and cupboards, and find a bundle of plastic shopping bags. One in particular catches my eye. The logo on the bag is red circles, immediately recognizable.

Holly considered herself lucky to get hired by Target. Unfortunately, it closed two years later. I think Holly would have preferred to talk about this with Grace. She was so nervous when she came over that day to ask for my help. Dressed in sweatpants and a sweatshirt, her hair pulled back into a ponytail. Her eyes were dark, made more pronounced by how pale her skin looked. She was visibly shaking. Her eyelids appeared to be heavy and her shoulders slumped.

"Dad, I am sorry to come here like this." Tears started sliding down her cheeks; her nose started to run and she grabbed for a tissue.

"Holly, what's going on? Are you all right? Are the boys okay?"

"The boys are fine."

"And you?"

"I'm . . . overwhelmed. I've been looking for work and there just isn't anything. Daniel will probably be going to college next year. I won't be able to help him with his expenses. I can't even afford to get his graduation photos at this point. It won't be long and Nathan will be going to college too."

"It takes time to find work. You have been doing your best. I can pay for the graduation photos. Don't worry about that."

"Dad, it isn't the graduation photos. I mean, it is, but there is more than that. . . I've seen a doctor."

"What did the doctor say?"

"She says that I should be put on a medication. It will help me feel better. She has diagnosed me with depression and anxiety." Her hands shake as she passes me a piece of paper.

"What is this?

"That is the medication she prescribed, as well as the price . . . per month."

$114.

"That is why I am here, Dad. I don't know what to do. I can't afford that."

"It's okay. I will give you the money."

"I didn't think you could afford it either."

"I will make it work. I want to know that you are okay, and if this will help, I will make it work." I gave her a hug then.

I have been helping her cover the cost of that medication ever since. I hope that she doesn't blame herself when she hears about my actions at the bank. It wasn't her fault, it was their fault—the bank should have offered more assistance in recovering the missing money. Sleep calls me to return to the comfort of the couch and awaiting blanket.

I wake up less confused. On my way out of the cottage, I gather my few belongings together and head out to my truck. It is early yet, and the roads are still quiet. With the steady

snowfall overnight, the roads are dicey. Driving the last of
Pigeon Lake Road and turning right onto Highway 36, I find
myself behind a plow. Ordinarily, this doesn't bother me—much
like farmers driving their tractors down the road, people tend to
be impatient with plow drivers. Today, I am in a hurry to get out
of town. When I stop for gas in Bobcaygeon, I hope to find a
map at the convenience store to help me decide where to go
next. The plow slowly makes its way down the road. I climb out
of my truck, closing the door behind me and fixing the collar of
my coat so that the cool wind doesn't give me a chill. Filling this
old truck has one drawback—it isn't cheap. The truck's gas tank
fills as the dollars continue to add up, when it finally stops, I
return the nozzle to its place and walk into the store. I look
around for maps, picking up one for Peterborough County, one
for Haliburton County, and another for Algonquin. Options, so I
can make an informed decision based on where I will be most
capable of forwarding the money to my daughter without
suspicion. Perusing the maps, I become aware of the car pulling
in beside my truck. The lights flicker across the paper in front of
me. This means my "plan" isn't going to work out.

The police officer looks at my truck and writes some notes in
a little book. His partner is just getting out of the car. I looked
around the store for another way out. Of course, in a tiny shop
like the ones at gas stations, there is no second exit available to
the public. I decide to go quietly. I resign myself to what is about
to happen and walk out the door to the police officer.

"Mr. Griffiths, do you know why my partner is examining
your truck?"

"I have a pretty good idea. I assume you are here to arrest
me."

"Yes, sir."

"All right. It's just, can you make sure that my daughter gets the envelope in my pocket?"

"Sir, everything on your person will be taken into custody and held as evidence."

The cuffs are cold against my skin. I am led out of the store and put into the back of the cruiser. A tear slides down my face. This time I am unable to wipe it away.

When we arrive at the police station, I have to turn over all my possessions. The envelope is secured in an evidence bag. My stomach twists and rolls with the emotions tormenting me. My mouth has gone dry. My legs do not offer the kind of stability I have come to expect over my lifetime. Included in the seizure of items is my wedding ring; before I drop that symbol of eternal love into the awaiting hand of the officer processing my arrest, I brush my lips across the gold surface. The officer allows me that moment of wistfulness.

Holly tries to contact me at the station, but I have requested to be left alone. I don't think I can bear the pain and concern in her eyes. I go through the motions of being put in a holding cell. I am given the number for Legal Aid.

HOLLY AND HER husband are sitting in the seats behind me; the public is welcome to watch the proceedings, so it doesn't surprise me much. I plead guilty and accept the sentence without appeal. I feel a hand on my shoulder and hear my daughter sniffling. I turn to face her. Before I leave the courtroom, I request that I have a photo of my family with me in my cell. Holly takes a picture out of her purse and passes it to me. Her eyes are wide with questions. She opens her mouth to speak, then closes it. I take the picture and look at it. My eyes start to sting. I feel the tears but hold them back. I quickly give hugs to my family. I can't offer any consolation beyond that; it isn't as though an explanation will make things better. When I am taken from the court house, the police load me into a car and drive to the Lindsay Superjail.

MY FIRST LETTER from Holly arrives, a white piece of paper folded in half:

Dad,

I hope that you are comfortable. I know, it's silly of me—jails aren't known for their hospitality. I am outside the courtroom while I write this, trying to make sense of what I just witnessed. My dad has been taken away, in handcuffs, to jail. My dad, a man I thought I knew. What could have possessed you to rob a bank? I just don't understand what happened . . .

Please, talk to me. I will come visit you. Mom would want us to stay in touch. She would want you to be home, to be in my life and in the lives of my children. I love you, Dad.

H.

After I finish reading the letter, I look at the slight depression and pale line across my skin, which will have to suffice in the absence of my wedding ring. Writing a response will have to wait until I am able to find the words. Grace would be so disappointed in my actions and in the way I have been ignoring Holly. Grace would have found another way, some other way of helping Holly. I know I've made a bad situation worse. I don't think I can fix things.

Dear Dad,

I have included some of your favourite cookies with this letter because I have great news. You will be so proud of your grandson. *Daniel has been accepted into Fleming College. He has also been informed that if he can maintain his average, he will be provided with a scholarship, which is renewable for each year of the program! Nathan has also been doing very well in school. He kept his grades in the 80s across the board. What smart boys I have brought into the world! Your grandsons are doing beautifully.*

I have a job. Starting next month, I will be a personal support worker. The hours will be long, but with the boys getting older, I feel that this has come at the right time. I am looking forward to starting this new chapter in my life. When you are released, you can move in with us. We have already moved many of your possessions here. We had to let most of your furniture go, though we kept all your bedroom furniture so that you would be comfortable. Our guest room now looks identical to your former master bedroom. I should also tell you that your wedding ring—and Mom's—is safe at home with me. The police released it to me last week. I have put it away for safekeeping until the day we can get it back on your finger where it belongs. I miss you, Dad. I wish you would let me come visit you.

Love,

Holly

I lie back on the thin mattress, smiling. My family will be all right. I ask a guard for a pencil and some paper. I need to write back. I scribble my letter quickly. My hand is shaky because I am overwhelmed by the wonderful news.

Dear Holly,

I know you are disappointed in me. I am disappointed in myself. I know I have hurt you. I appreciate that you haven't held this against me. Instead, you have kept me up to date with all the news from home. Your mother is smiling down on your family, happy in all the good that has happened as of late. I am so proud of you and your sons. Please tell the boys congratulations.

Thank you for taking care of my things, moving them into your home. I hope that it wasn't a terrible inconvenience. Please, take the wedding rings, see what money you can get for them. I want to know that you are all right. That is all that I have ever wanted, to know that my family is safe, healthy, and happy.

I am sorry that I have kept my distance, but I believe it has been for the best. I love you.
—Dad

Grace returns to my thoughts, though she is never truly far from them, then my eyes close and I drift into a peaceful slumber, from which I do not wake.

A WEEK LATER . . .

A letter is delivered to Holly's address. The envelope has a return address indicating it comes from the financial institution involved in Mr. Griffith's case.

Dear Mr. Griffiths,

I apologize for the time it has taken for our investigation to determine the whereabouts of your missing funds. We did a thorough inspection of your expenses and the amount of money you regularly spent each month. It is our finding that while using our online banking website, a hacker accessed your information, likely the result of an unprotected PC. The hacker seems to have transferred the funds through a number of accounts, making it impossible to track. We recommend that in future you update your internet security. Some suggestions are:

- Make sure to password-protect your Wi-Fi connection

- Install internet security with anti-phishing

- Keep internet security and computer up to date

- Ensure that our website begins with https:// before you enter your information

- Never access your accounts over an open or unsecured Wi-Fi connection

It is with deepest regrets that we must inform you that we would have been able to return a portion up to 50% of the money stolen, under the condition of our insurance. As the funds were misappropriated while under your control and on your network, we would have been unable to provide a full refund. Given the extenuating circumstances, that of your criminal activity in one of our branches, our legal representation is currently working with the insurance company to determine whether this refund should still be available to you. We hope that this matter will be fully resolved in the coming months. If you would like to contest any of our findings, feel free to speak to your own counsel.

Mr. Arthur Grand, Bank Manager

***

Tiffany Short is a self-proclaimed creative nerd. She is an avid reader with several creative outlets. In terms of her education background, Tiffany pursued a Bachelor of Arts (Honours) degree in English prior to earning a Bachelor of Education. Since November 2015, she has been participating in the Circle of Writers group at the Kawartha Lakes library in Lindsay, and as of March 2016, she has started a writing mentorship with Sylvia McNicoll offered by CSARN. Tiffany is currently working on a novel as part of her mentorship.

UNREASONABLE

Altaire Gural

"YOU'RE AT THE Murder House, aren't you?"

The cashier is smiling at me with more enthusiasm than I think should be allowed, and I guess I'm frowning, because she starts to stutter. "I'm sorry. Sorry. I guess I just thought . . . It's just nice that . . . that there's finally a family in that old house, you know?"

These small towns, they freak me out. Everyone knows everyone, and somehow they all find comfort in that. I'm loading my groceries into the back of my truck and trying to hurry because people keep nodding and smiling at me. And it's weird. I guess you can't really hide in a small town. Shit.

We've been renting an old farmhouse for about two weeks now, and while it lacks the distinct charm a century farmhouse usually has—no six-paned windows, no creeping ivy, no wishing well—it's spacious and it's private. And it's peaceful. God, it's so quiet. I still wake up in a panic most nights, but thankfully it's not for any specific reason, just the absolute lack of urban noise.

Later on I'm in the kitchen making a very basic spaghetti dinner, a salad, nothing fancy. My kids come running down the stairs.

"Oooh, garlic bread! Excellent! Mom, can you tell Ella to stop going into my room and leaving the light on? It's driving me nuts."

"Jesus, Jerk. It's not me," Ella manages around a mouthful of the garlic bread she's snarfed. The decibel level of this argument reaches Wagner-like heights, and I'm done with it. I have little patience these days.

"Ella, don't touch the lights in his room."

"It's not me!" Ella protests. "Anyways, tell Josh to stop closing my bedroom door. That is *also* irritating."

"Fine. All things belonging to the opposite-gendered sibling

—off limits. Indefinitely. Are we good?" Neither kid is satisfied with the lack of winning, and there is mutiny in their weak agreements that leads me to believe I have likely now failed at garnering some checkmark on the parenting board. Ah well. Over the course of dinner, however, hostilities give way to laughing. It's been so long since we've laughed at a dinner table. I'd almost forgotten what it was like to hear my kids laugh. Fuck it. I'm not going to cry here. I don't want Ella and Josh to think anything is wrong. Anything else, anyway. School tomorrow, I remind them. Great. The mutiny is back. First day at a new school and I refuse to worry. These kids can handle it.

They've been in bed for hours and I still can't sleep. I cave and open up Facebook. Double-edged sword, this Facebook. Several messages of "Where are you?" Delete. "Jason's freaking out." Delete. "Are you ok?" *I'm fine.* Delete. Delete delete delete. I'm more than okay. I'm free. *Tell Jason nothing,* I remind them. *Say nothing.* I click through the rest of the updates, read a few articles (note to self: stop reading such heavy-duty articles). I play a few games of Bejeweled Blitz. I determine the be-all and end-all of my existence with such affirming oracles as What Flower Are You? and Who Were You In A Past Life? and What Do Your Eyes Say About You? . . . What Is Your Spirit Animal? is especially on point tonight. Fuck's sake, how did we ever self-identify before Facebook came along? What Myers-Briggs Type Are You? INFP. Yeah, no shit. Whether my introversion is natural or whether it was forced upon me, it's here to stay now; I prefer the distance between myself and all avenues of shame and pain—thanks, friends. Screen time only is a connection that suits me fine.

I swear I just heard a woman's voice in my ear. I stop scrolling and tilt my head. A weird whispering, definitely a woman, but I can't make out what she's saying. And then it's gone. A quick screen check tells me it's actually three twenty in the morning and I should really get my ass to bed. After all, I remind myself, lack of sleep makes people delusional.

"You turned my light on again!"

"Well you closed my door."

"I can't sleep with the light on! Mom!"

I love them dearly, but I am counting the minutes till the school bus gets here.

WHY IS THE house so bloody cold? I really should go into town and order propane, but it's only September. Instead I go to the shed to get firewood. As I make my way back to the house, I freeze. There's a man standing in the driveway. I drop the firewood, my heart running right the fuck out of my chest, but when I look back there is no one there. I slowly count to ten, catch my breath and calm down, pick up the firewood, and return to the house. Fuck it. I'm going into town. *You're just imagining yard silhouettes,* I tell myself. It's the country; that kind of cheap trash kitsch would be logical on my front lawn. *Stop being such a paranoid twit.*

"Can I help you?" The lady at the propane service desk smiles that friendly smile I am seriously growing to distrust. *I don't deserve your smiles.* "Propane. Smart of you to order now when the prices are lower, that's for sure. Can I have your address?" When I tell her where I live, she goes ghost white and chokes back a weird, breathy gulp. Before I can ask her if she's all right, she volunteers, "That was my friend Karen's house. She . . . passed away several years ago."

I don't know how to respond to this. "Come have tea sometime" seems wildly inappropriate. I manage an "I'm sorry" and practically flee out to the parking lot. This. Fucking. Town. I don't want to know everybody.

When the kids get home they're vibrating with more awesome news. "Guess what this house is called?" Josh bellows. "The Murder House! Can you believe it? The Murder House. Ho. Lee. shit."

"Watch your language," I warn him. *And thanks, local school kids, you're a total help.*

"Mom," Ella cuts in. "A woman was murdered in this house. With Josh's lights, and my door always closing . . . What if we have a ghost?"

What if we do?

After the kids are in bed, I decide to look this story up on Google. Yup. There it is. Karen Rivers, aged thirty-six. History of suffering domestic violence and ultimately killed by her ex-husband, stabbed while she was in her kitchen (my kitchen). Her two teenage children managed to escape out the upper bedroom window (Ella's room) and run across the back fields to the neighbour's house. There was a police pursuit, and the ex-husband was killed when his car hit a spike belt and flipped over.

God.

More searching reveals the children are now in their twenties, one not doing so well in a nearby town, the other struggling to raise a young family.

I sit in my chair, just staring out the window for what seems like ages, trying to process. *Are you there?* I address the space around me. *Are you checking on my kids? Is that why you turn lights on, and close Ella's door?*

With all due respect to the prospective ghost, I think I've done an admirable job of looking after my kids. Well, recently, anyway.

I don't want to feel connected to Karen Rivers, but I do. I don't want to see the parallels, but they're there. The irony is not lost on me that that woman's loss turns out to be my safe haven. I keenly feel the pain of her not being there to watch her children grow up. Not being able to protect them, prepare them for the world. I empathize. I want to cry for her. Aren't ghosts omnipresent? Doesn't she know about her kids? Is that way she's checking in on mine?

I start talking out loud to her most nights, after the kids have gone to bed. "Are you homesick?" I ask her. I understand why she might not want to leave, and I lie and tell her her own children are doing just fine. Wouldn't she want to hear that? I thank her every night too. "Thank you for watching over my children." I get used to the cold spots in the living room, and the non-specific whispering. Ella doesn't. More than once I've found her downstairs, sleeping on the couch that she's pulled out into the middle of the wooden floor, a circle of salt surrounding her makeshift bed. I keep having to buy more boxes of Sifto.

"I think the ghost is homesick," I tell Ella.

Then I think to ask Ella if she misses our old home in the city too.

"Home is where you are Mom. As long as we're together, it's home. I can't be homesick." Okay, that just about brings me to my knees, and I turn to look out the window so Ella won't catch me crying. It's true. Home is where my children are.

Yes, you're homesick, Karen.

"NO ONE'S SEEN or heard from Jason for days."

I stare at the message, kind of hypnotized, snake-charmed. I guess that's appropriate. More messages in my inbox saying very nearly the same thing, from several people. I know why they're telling me, but really, why can't they keep that to themselves? I want to scream and throw the monitor, but it's late, and also I can't afford another monitor.

New message from Unknown Sender: *r u ok r u ok r u ok r u ok r u ok r u ok r u ok r u ok r u ok*

What the hell?

The room is positively frigid, so I get up to get my shawl, but as I pass the kitchen window there is an orange flashing interrupting the absolute dark outside. My truck hazards are blinking. I know the truck is locked, and that the keys are hanging right there on the key hook by the door, because I can see them. My heart is pounding so hard my chest actually hurts, but I go out to do a cursory check anyway. Yup. Truck is locked. It's quiet as tombs out here. Nothing.

I have chaotic, angry dreams all night. I think it's Karen I see, in my kitchen, trying to calm a desperate man. She's polite, she's compassionate, she's crying. I see her children climbing out the window (Ella's window), sobbing as they trip along the ruts in the furrowed field behind the house, holding hands as they run to the neighbour's.

There's no reasoning. There's no reasoning with him.

The words are never spoken, but the message is etched in my brain. I wake up crying, my heart broken for that family. "I'm sorry," I whisper to the empty air.

THE FIRE IS popping in the wood stove and we're playing an epic game of Settlers of Catan. Ella's giggling is infectious, and Josh and I can't help but laugh too. This is how home feels.

He's here.

I startle at the clarity of the voice in my ear. The kids notice my abrupt change in demeanour, my eyes wide. Despite the fire, the room is freezing.

There is no reasoning.

I get up to look out the window. There is a man standing in the driveway. This time it is no shadowy figure. It's Jason. I'm frozen only for an instant.

"Upstairs," I order the kids, and they don't question. We used to argue with our fear all the time, reason ourselves out of it, and what we knew. Not this time.

As I hear the doorknob rattling in the front hall we are racing up the stairs to Ella's bedroom. Out the window, across the back field. We run for the neighbours.

I hear you, Karen. There is no reasoning.

I'm holding my children's hands as we run, and I do not let go.

***

Altaire Gural, a member of the Playwrights Guild of Canada, has published poetry, short stories, plays, and magazine editorials. She is currently working on a YA novel based on her fantasy play *Forgotten*, a reimagining of what happened after Neverland that has been performed in Canada, the U.K., and the United States, and has successfully won entrance into several juried festivals.

BEANS

Cathy Hamill-Hill

THANK GOD FOR for my guinea pigs. I can see light from my east window, so it must be morning. Those pigs have to be fed every morning and every night. I know what they want, too. I give them fresh beans; those pigs love beans.

Ouch, ouch, ouch. Everything hurts this morning. The leg I broke twenty years ago, falling off a bale in the barn, feels like it broke again, but it is just that arthritis. Arthritis hurts like the dickens. The arm I sprained two summers ago when I grabbed the ladder as I fell doesn't feel good either. More arthritis in that arm, too. And darn, there goes my stomach again. I wish my stomach would stop hurting like that; makes me wonder what it is as it hurts so much sometimes. Now, where are my glasses? Oh, I better put those stupid teeth in too. Yuck, that cleaning stuff tastes awful, but I do feel more like me with them on. And I better get the hearing aid on if I can find it. Yes, here it is, that buzzing sound makes me think of a hundred bees, but now it is okay- have to remember to turn that part off. Now I need to find some underwear; have to put that on today too. I have to look as decent and as young as possible—a lot depends on today. I do not want to leave this farm, and I don't want trouble.

I love this farm. I love owning a piece of country here in the Kawartha Lakes. This is the only home I have ever known. This farm might not look as great as it once did, but it still looks good in my opinion. I love the barn most. The barn is huge. Once, we had milk cows, sheep, draft horses, and a big henhouse. Now, I just have some sheep and goats. And I have Charlie the Lab, a mutt dog I found slinking around the front porch. My dad gave this farm to me.

God, you know how much I loved Dad. Sure, to many he was a "deaf and dumb" old man, but in truth, he was more chatty then a box of mad chipmunks. He could grunt a full sentence, and he could sign fast as lightning in his own way. I know, "farm sign" is not the proper sign language taught in schools; we had our own. He bought this farm from doing jobs nobody else would do. He was often hired to dig out overflowing septic systems. These systems were new to the area back then, and people forgot they had to be cleaned out at least once every ten years with twelve people using them in an average household. He would come home smelling so bad that he would greet me with his two fingers pegged on his nose—and point toward the sky. That meant he was going to strip outside and run into the shower, and I was supposed to go upstairs and close my bedroom door. When I heard water running, I would go outside and pick up his clothes with a stick—sometimes I had to burn them in a barrel, they were so bad. Nobody cared how rough the job was for the "deaf" guy. One time, I made a nice supper and pretended I cooked it over the barrel that was burning Dad's clothes—I laughed so hard at the way he dropped his fork. I still laugh to this day when I think about it.

I loved my dad, and sometimes I think he's still here with me. I can see him smiling when I go to the barn and tend to the animals just like he did. I even wear my dad's barn coat, even though it's way too big for me. It still smells like Dad did; it smells like barn, and it still has patches of ground-in soil from when he was planting beans the last spring he was here.

This farm is beautiful. It is nestled in the Kawartha Lakes—actually, it was Victoria County, but now it's the City of Kawartha Lakes, and that sounds even better. We are just outside of Lorneville, north of Woodville. I am right in the middle of nowhere, but it is everywhere to me. Every corner of this place holds memories for me, and I don't want to move to no city.

I hear the car—excuse me, the SUV. Mark is crazy for having the best. Mark is my son. Well, sort of. He really is my distant cousin, but I think he's my son and he thinks he's my son, so we leave it at that. Back in my day, we just did what we had to do and kept our mouths shut. Dad's cousin was more than grateful to get rid of Mark—she wanted to get rid of him before he was born, but Dad begged her not to.

Oh, thank God, false alarm.

That was the milk truck going next door to Luke's farm. I'm still early; thank God again.

Okay, got to find some clean clothes, preferably something of this decade. There, that looks new; actually, it is new. "Feel the spirit in the City," says the logo on that shirt I bought last week with Luke; I forgot about that. Gives Mark a good jab, too. I love my City of Kawartha Lakes. Now, some pants—nope, not them. Yuck, I better hide those. No way Mark would understand that the manure on these pants is gold—thought for sure that lamb would die, and when it went all over my pants, I just smiled, as then I knew the bowels were working finally.

Speaking of bowels, I know where I need to go soon. I better swallow a bottle of something to quiet them down when I'm done. If Mark hears me again making "fluffy sounds," as he calls a loud ripper, I'll get in trouble again. It is not like I meant to when that real estate guy was here, it just was that I had baked beans for dinner and supper the day before. Dad and I use to have so much fun with beans . . . He called it the "perfume food," and he would laugh and laugh when I nearly made the kitchen green with stink. The doctor said I should not eat beans, but Dad said I should; he could grown beans on this farm by the bushel, so he said it was our "native perfume." I didn't eat beans the last five days, but today I'm so nervous. I feel all tense. I'm so scared of what might happen today.

There, I'm ready. The guinea pigs are fed and watered. I'm wearing clean clothes. I'm empty except for that stuff I just took to settle my stomach. I sure wish my stomach would quit hurting, but at least it will be quiet. I have all my "extra parts" on. Clara did my hair yesterday, so I'm afraid to even touch it. She loaded it in spray so it feels like cement, but she says it is guaranteed to look good for today. I had Luke come in to do the chores to be sure everything is done perfectly. He just called in to say the sheep, goats, and Charlie all look real good today. Luke put down extra straw, too, so everything looks like a picture. Luke turned my truck around too and parked it by the house, so it looks like it was parked carefully; he lined it up just like I asked.

Luke is my gift from God. He's a neighbour boy. Well, he's not a boy, he's fifty-two years old, but he's a boy to me. He really likes beans. He can do anything, and I can't do much these days, but only Luke knows that. I give him enough money to be sure he keeps my secrets. I tell him it's "shhhh money." He says with the amount I give him, he doesn't even know my name, much less anything else. I know what Luke used to do and nobody else does; no wonder I trust him. If people knew that Luke was a child arsonist they would have him kicked out of here so fast. He told me he burned down five barns, so now he's determined to own five barns and keep them in perfect condition to pay back for his past sins, he says.

I better take another breath here and try to look calm. Oh, please God, let me keep this farm. I just can't leave the City of Kawartha Lakes. I love it here. I love the seasons. . . the snowy winters. "Mud," which is what I call spring, since I have Charlie the Lab, who loves walking in mud. The warm summers mean the fresh beans and hay coming in. Harvest or autumn or fall here in the Kawartha Lakes is a season that can't be nicer. The Lindsay Fair, the Bobcaygeon Fair, the Oakwood Fair—three events that make my blood tingle with joy. For over fifty years we have entered beans in the vegetable division, and for the last fifty years we have won first prize. We won again last year. Last year, when I walked around the fair with Luke, I felt like I was five years old again. When the judge came over and pinned that red ribbon on Dad's vest that I was wearing at the end of the day, I was crying happy tears. I couldn't, thankfully, see the stares from people as Luke held my old hand like a teenager, but I could feel them; not that we cared.

Oh, God, help me. I hear Mark's SUV . . . and then I hear her voice too.

I hate her. She's the hoity-toity female from the city, not "my" city, but that other city. She's coming to evaluate me, as if I'm property that she wants to sell. She is one of those "workers" that decide if old people can live by themselves or not. Mark can't stand the idea of me living here alone on a farm, and he just wants this place sold and me boxed up.

"Hi, Mommy!" says Mark as he comes into my house. He kisses me, and I nearly fall over under his stink of something fake.

"Hi, dear," I say in my sweetest voice. I hope I sound strong.

"Well, Ms. Rowlands, I will get right to business here, if you don't mind," says the hoity-toity one, clicking her long nails. If I had a sheep with nails that long, I would be calling in Luke to get them trimmed.

"Certainly, Miss Tyline," I say with my best voice. "I don't want to take any more of your time than I have to." I answer just like I practiced with Charlie last night after me and Luke got this house cleaned up.

"This place sure looks good, Mom," Mark says as he moves around. I can't see exactly what he's doing, since he's across the room, but I know there is nothing for me to be scared about. Luke and I moved anything that he could consider "weird," like my stash of weed that I put in muffins when I hurt really bad. We made sure that any papers were safe from Mark's eyes. Luke must have vacuumed a dozen times to get Charlie's fur off the rug.

"Ms. Rowlands, we have assessed your situation here. I've talked to your doctors and we reviewed the medical files," Hoity-Toity says.

"So, can I stay in my home?" I break in. Darn, I meant to be calm and strong, not desperate! I feel like kicking myself; in fact, I feel that way now as I can feel something huge starting to build in me. I chew on a bean to calm myself down.

"Ms. Rowlands, you are ninety-three years old. You are a single female living in the country, all alone, and you have already fallen many times. This place is so isolated. There are such nice places for you to live near Mark. We have found two great ones for you. One even has a cat! We have—"

"I'm not alone! I have my animals! This is my home; I know every corner, every—"

"Ms. Rowlands, your heart tests came back, and they are not good. I just feel that for your own—"

I honestly didn't mean to do it. But when you have a cup of cold tea near your good hand and someone is telling you that you have to leave your home, you just kind of lose it. I throw the whole thing in her face.

"Mother!" roars Mark. I tried to hold it back. It just

wouldn't stop.

My heart tests? Now it's my heart too? The doctor didn't even check out this stomach I have now. It looks like I'm going to go, just like Dad. If I'm lucky. I do wish Mark and Hoity-Toity would just leave.

I stand up and flip on the light switch for the outside light when nobody is looking.

"How could you?" shrieks Mark, as the hoity-toity one totters in her high heels toward the bathroom, screaming like I threw hot fire in her face. Mark sits down beside me so close I can see him, of course; I can smell him too, and he still smells way too strong. I try not to gag.

"Mother, listen to me! That's it. You are not staying here. You are leaving this forsaken place and moving to the real city with me—"

"No, I'm not," I tell him, and I mean it.

I know I can't reason with Mark. He's so mad he's vibrating. I make an excuse to go to the bathroom; that's one place he won't follow me. Mark never gets his hands dirty. He was so clean when he was young that every birthday we got him soap and white towels, as he was always washing his hands.

I can barely see the steps, but I know where to put my feet, and I hang on tight to the railing that Luke put in for me when I had a fall last week. Thank God Mark never knew Luke came in and found me sprawled on the floor. I just slipped down one step, so I didn't break anything. Luke wanted me to go to the hospital, but I knew as soon as I got there, Mark would be called and there would go my home.

I'm now in the bathroom, the downstairs one, but what I'm really doing is going to the barn from the side door. I flush the toilet and run some water to make it sound good. Luke is going to meet me in the barn, as the light on means Plan B is required. Luke is going to drive me to the Lindsay Town Hall for two o'clock. Clara and her husband will be there too, along with a preacher.

Luke and I have to get married. We are going to be married as friends and he will get every single thing I own. I know I haven't got long left, but Luke will care for me until I have to go into palliative care in Ross Memorial Hospital in Lindsay. It won't be long, judging by the way my stomach hurts today. I don't want to burden Luke, but what choice do I have? I cannot bear leaving Kawartha Lakes, ever. I want to stay with Dad and have our ashes spread together, right here. I promised Dad I would never leave this farm, and I meant it.

Now that I'm in the barn, I feel peace. My sheep and goats rustle in the fresh straw. Faint snores mean the animals are having their usual morning naps after their breakfast. The light is bright against the windows to the west, meaning this day is half done. I walk, carefully, further down the hall and see a shadow. Luke turns out to be the shadow, and he moves in real close so I can see him. I tell Luke that Mark is trying to get rid of me and he wants to sell the place. Luke opens his arms wide and I step into them. It is nice and safe against Luke.

Luke grins and hands me a bean. Charlie the lab comes bounding over to us, and he too has a bean in his mouth. We all eat beans. Charlie wags his tail, and Luke signs, "We are happy friends."

I hear the house door and frantically sign to Luke, "Mark come!"

Luke's truck is parked so close to the barn that he grabs my hand and literally pushes me into the cab. I slide across the bench seat and already we are racing to the Lindsay Town Hall in Luke's truck. My heart is beating so fast that all I can do is pray it doesn't stop now. I look over at Luke and see him looking intently at the road and at the rearview mirror. I know, without seeing, what he's looking at—it has to be Mark and Hoity-Toity.

This truck of Luke's is really nice. It must be new, or he must have cleaned it for today. It smells like lemons, and I like this leather seating. I'm glad I wore nice clothes today. This is not a barn coat kind of truck. I hang on as we go faster and faster.

We get to the Lindsay Town Hall a few minutes ahead of Mark. Luke parks the truck in front of the back door just like we planned. We rush to the office to find everybody standing in place. It is two o'clock.

By the time Mark gets parked and finds us, it's over. I'm married, and Luke legally owns it all. Luke can't hear a word, and my hearing aids are in my pocket. I don't need hearing aids with Luke. I've never seen Mark this mad before. He is a shade of purple, and Hoity-Toity looks about the same colour; they both could do with some Kawartha Lakes sunshine. Security comes and gets Mark and her out. I wave at them. Clara and her husband wave too, and we all laugh.

We are ready to go back home. Luke holds my hand in the truck and smiles over at me three times. My chest hurts, my right arm hurts, and my stomach hurts, but inside my mind I'm as happy as I was with Dad. I love the scenery we pass: the fields of wheat that look like sheets of gold that come right to the road so I can see them good. I love the trees along the road all dressed in autumn, and I'm grateful that the winds didn't come so they have their full dresses on for us on our wedding day. Kawartha Lakes is the most beautiful place on this side of the sky, I'm sure.

Now, I have Charlie here eating beans, and Luke is outside

picking more beans because the guinea pigs are hungry again. I've thawed out a bean casserole for tonight, because that is what I want for my last supper.

***

Cathy Hamill-Hill was a baby who wailed until she was taken outside to be with her dad at the family's fifth-generation barn. Her writing career began with a little story about goats in a deceased newspaper. She married Mr. Hill, whom she calls "Sweetie" and who owned an acreage in Cannington where he built her a barn. Her writing works span from agriculture, municipal politics, community events, and minutes for the church board. Cathy works for Kawartha Lakes Public Library and *Voice of the Farmer*. Showing tortoiseshell/white guinea pigs at local fairs with camera in hand is her self-confessed addiction.

It's Not The Fleas Or The Ticks

Lori Rowsell

MISS NELLY FLOOD, Luce's third-grade teacher, was the first to know. She knew everything before anyone else on account of her father being Edward Flood of the *Victoria Warder*. All of the ladies and tittle-tats in the county followed her around like she was a mother goose—even though most of them were twice her age—hoping to be the second to catch wind of any gossip. One morning, while Miss Flood was smack dab in the middle of the book of Job, one such gosling burst through the double doors of the schoolhouse and shouted, "Nelly, say it isn't so. Has the ague truly come to Purdy's Mills?"

Of course Miss Flood had already told her students that the ague was moving its way across the county and that anyone with a cough or fever was to go home immediately to prevent getting anyone else sick. Their schoolhouse was impressive enough in terms of physical size, but no amount of trying was going to keep the ague from spreading like dust in a windstorm should anyone carry it through the front doors. No one got up to leave, no one so much as sniffled, but Luce was getting mighty bored with Job and seized the opportunity to enjoy a quiet afternoon at home. Plus she already knew all about the ague anyhow. Mr. Flood paid her a nickel to deliver a bundle of papers to the baker, the post office, the general store, and the hardware store every morning before school for the past six months.

Luce shuffled through the doors behind the ladies, trying to look sick. "Miss Flood. My cheeks are warm and I feel a fit coming on. I think I ought to go home."

The gosling jumped back as if Luce stuck her with a hot poker, and cowered behind Miss Flood.

"Certainly, Luce. Do you need an escort?"

Knowing they'd be watching her every step, Luce feigned a sick-walk as long as she could stand to and called out feebly,

"No, thank you, Miss Flood. I can walk myself just fine."

"You be sure to go right home and tell your mama straight away," Miss Flood called out after Luce, who waved and set off at a decent pace once she'd rounded the corner out of view.

When Luce reached her home—a twenty-minute walk on dry ground, but twice that long if it had been raining—she discovered her mother in a panic. Mother announced that people were dying from the ague, it wasn't going to pass through this time, and inspected her daughter roughly, pulling at her ears and prying down her eyelids. Then she unleashed a flurry of questions.

"Are you sick? Why have you come home from school so early? Did Miss Flood send everyone home?" And then, remembering who Luce's teacher was, and that her daughter had most certainly read the *Warder* before delivering it, one hand shot to her throat while the other hovered an inch from her middle; a strangled sound escaped her lips. "Has something else happened? How many more are sick?"

Luce's ears burned hot for having to admit she'd lied about being sick so she could leave school early on purpose. Mother looked so angry that Luce thought she might strike her.

"I'm sorry, Mother. I'm quite simply sick to death of Job." Mother flinched at the reference and Luce tried again. "We've read Job a hundred times. I know it inside out and backward. I don't know why we can't take turns reading the *Warder*. At least the news changes day to day. Job is always the same. Did you know that Mr. Purdy and his boys are planning a grist mill?"

"Luce!"

"I'm sorry, Mother. And Walter Flavelle next to me—you know the Flavelle boy—well, he was itching and fidgeting in his seat all morning. He's probably got fleas again, and I couldn't take another damn minute of it."

Mother kissed her daughter's forehead, her long hair tickling Luce's nose. After a long moment, Mother released her daughter and warned her to mind her tongue to prevent father from plucking it out. Luce tried, unsuccessfully, not to laugh at her mother's empty threat, and dashed over the stairs to her room. The afternoon sun was pulsing a wave of heat through Luce's bedroom window, resulting in a sweltering difference between the temperature on either side of her bedroom door. It was so warm and bright that she couldn't help but crawl under the rays of sunshine and fall into a fast, deep sleep.

WHEN LUCE FINALLY awakened, the air was cool and dark. She'd been covered up to her chin with a white sheet and her window opened. Between the moonlight from the open window and a barely burning lamp on the bedside table, a nightmare of shadows blanketed the room. Luce had seen her room by moonlight nearly every night for as long as she could remember, but somehow, that night it was different. Luce decided that she must have gone and got herself struck by heat in the sweltering afternoon sun, and sat up to rub the sleep from her eyes. It wasn't until one of the shadows—a tall, animal-like shape— stepped off the wall and stalked across the room that Luce realized she wasn't alone. A long black tail caressed the doorframe and disappeared into the hall.

Mother and Father were seated in the living room. Father's shirt was undone to the waist, as was often the case when he and Mother were in a sour mood with each other, and he raked his fingers, white-knuckled, through his hair as if considering ripping it out from the roots. Mother was seated quietly on the chair opposite him, silent and staring blankly into the fire. It was likely that Mr. Connolly was late paying his rent. Again. Luce watched them for a moment and decided that whatever was bothering them, it was best to leave them undisturbed.

The shadow Luce had followed into the hallway meowed and wrapped itself around her ankles to capture her attention. Not wanting to alert Mother and Father to her presence on the stairs, Luce silenced it with a little kick. It wouldn't bode well to disturb them when they were in a foul mood. The cat leapt silently down the stairs and Luce followed it, careful to avoid the spots she knew would groan in protest under her newly acquired weight. She'd grown a full three inches since the start of school, and those three inches were heavy enough to make the stairs creak every time.

The screen door blew open wide, having caught a gust of air when the cat pushed through, and Luce startled at the sound of Mother's bare feet slapping across the wooden floor behind her. Luce stole after the cat, knocking that morning's edition of the *Warder* to the ground in her wake. She peeked over the windowsill and saw Mother crying as she collected the overturned pages. Luce settled into the grass below the window, feeling somewhat guilty about upsetting the paper, and waited patiently until Mother pulled the door shut. The black cat occupied itself with trapping lightning bugs under its paws in the uncut grass.

"Psst! I hope you aren't going to eat that," Luce whispered, her tone near scolding. "One time, I brought Mother home a present, a whole jar of lightning bugs, but she made me set them loose. They're poisonous."

The cat challenged Luce with green marbles eyes and flicked its tail, seemingly annoyed. It released the bug from under its paws and sauntered lazily across the lawn to sit at her feet.

"I wasn't going to eat it," the cat said, lapping a shine onto its coat under the moon light.

Luce frowned, trying to pinpoint the moment she should have realized she was dreaming. By rights it should have been the moment she awakened and realized she'd slept through supper. Mother would have never let her sleep through supper.

"What's the matter? Haven't you seen a cat before?"

"Of course I've seen a cat before. In fact, I've always wanted a pet, but Father is allergic and Mother says they wreck the curtains."

The cat threw itself to the ground and bawled in protest. "Why is it always about the curtains?"

It was a pathetic display, and Luce let a silly giggle escape in return. She reached out to tickle the cat's belly, then pulled her hand back sharp in case Mother was still standing at the window.

"Don't worry," said the cat. "She can't see you from where she's standing."

A stray fire bug fluttered by and landed on the cat's nose, seemingly unaware of any potential danger. The cat shook its head, fighting the temptation to eat it, and instead gingerly attacked the hem of Luce's nightgown.

"Hey!"

"Do you want to play with me?" asked the cat.

Luce nodded excitedly and the cat took off at lightning speed, outracing even the fire bugs. Luce had never played with a cat before, let alone one that could speak, so she followed the cat through a narrow part in the bush at the far corner of the yard.

"What are we going to play?" she said, trying to keep up with the nimble cat. "I'm afraid I don't know any cat games."

"We could always go back for your mother's curtains."

Luce gasped, slightly offended, but enjoying the cat's humour. "You're a naughty kitty."

"Perhaps we can play hide and seek. There are plenty of hiding spots here."

At the end of the narrow path, between the part in the bushes at the far corner of the yard, was the "here" the cat was referring to. It was an old cemetery. Luce had been there many times before. She came to the cemetery when she wanted to be alone, which was most often when she was fed up with school or chores. Sometimes she simply needed to escape her shouting parents. It was peaceful and quiet, except for bird songs and butterfly kisses, but they were never a bother   though she'd never been there after dark. The moon was so high in the sky that there was ample light on the burial plots themselves, but the shadows were deep at the edge of the trees, and Luce wondered if any of them might get up and walk off like the cat had done in her bedroom. Mother had told her once that Purdy's pioneers were buried there and that they were lucky to have them on their land. Luce wasn't so sure.

"You don't have to be afraid here," said the cat, as if Luce had spoken her fears aloud. "I'll count and you hide."

The cat lowered its head to the ground and covered its green eyes with giant paws. Its butt and tail stuck up in the air, waving slightly back and forth with the rhythm of his counting. Luce looked around; there were many places one could hide—about that, the cat was right—but the faces of the stones prevented her from seeking one.

In the daylight, Luce had read every single name on every stone aloud. She'd even placed flowers on some of them when it would have been their birthday, but now the writing on the stones was blurry, obscured by a gently rolling fog that was thick

102

and clung to the rock surfaces like icing. She was only vaguely aware when the cat stopped counting and perched itself atop the headstone in front of her.

"Why can't I see it proper?"

"You will. Be patient." The cat jumped down and swept its tail across her bare arm, tickling it. "Want to see something?"

Luce nodded.

The cat dove in to a cloud of fog and disappeared from view, only to poke its head back up ten feet away. His floating, bodyless head bobbed up and down in the fog, producing a rolling laughter from Luce's lips.

"Okay, okay," she said, gulping down the foggy air to settle her hiccoughs. "This time I'll hide for real. You count again."

The cat disappeared below the fog. This time only his tail poked through the fog, tall and sturdy like a mountain peak.

The pair played hide and seek for what felt like hours. They'd used up all the good hiding places at least twice each, and Luce had even dressed one of the headstones in her white nightgown, leaving it a near-glowing beacon under the pale moonlight. Then Luce remembered the best hiding spot, one where Father could never find her and Mother was too afraid to find in case there should be spiders. It was behind an old hidden door in her bedroom closet. Luce ran as hard as she could through the narrow path back toward the house. The path hadn't been wet with mud on the way through the bush the first time, but it had been known to rain on one end of town but not the other.

A picture of said event was even published in the *Warden* on the front page. Bryan Hutton was paid twenty cents for it, and after that Edward Flood's office was nearly drowned with photos of fat-faced babies laced with bonnets from mothers hoping to also be paid such a sum.

When Luce reached the part in the bush at the other end of the trail, she was frozen in place by the light. The midday sun was high in the sky, yet in the graveyard not one hundred yards away, it was still the middle of night. The cat came at a tear through the part in the bush and collided with the back of Luce's legs.

"Luce, come on. Let's go back now. I'll bet the fog has lifted and we can read the headstones."

"Am I still dreaming?" Luce asked the cat.

"You're not dreaming, Luce. Now come with me. It's time to go," the cat said, his voice stern.

"But I know a good hiding spot. You'll never find me. Count again and I'll hide."

Having already forgotten the strangeness of sudden day, Luce blew through the screen door of the house like a wayward wind, intent on hiding where the cat would never find her. She climbed the stairs two at a time and kicked open her bedroom door to a nearly unrecognizable space. There were no sheets on her bed, and she didn't remember seeing them hanging on the line. The bed had also been moved to the middle of the room flanked by two lonely chairs, one on either side.

Boxes were piled haphazardly in front of the secret door, preventing Luce from climbing in. The cat appeared at Luce's mud-soaked feet, nimbly avoiding the mess himself.

"Oh no, Mother's coming," Luce whispered loudly. "She's going to be so angry about the mud." Luce turned in circles, unable to leave her room, or she'd surely be found out, so she followed the cat under the bed. She could hear both Mother's and Father's footsteps barrelling over the stairs. Luce was certain they must have found the mess.

"I know what I heard. It was her," said Mother, her voice

hoarse.

Father growled an impatient sigh. "That's impossible. She isn't here."

"I can *feel* her. And look. Footprints."

Mother was crying and Luce was tempted to come out from under the bed and accept her punishment, but she was frozen with fear.

"You must have tracked it in when you were stripping the bed," said Father.

Mother stamped on the floor and raised her voice. "I did no such thing. I don't know why and I don't know how, but she is here and these are her footprints. Luce is in this house."

"Goddamn it, Carol. Would you get a hold of yourself? She isn't coming back."

Father stomped out of the room, slamming the door behind him, and Mother cried for a long time before she was able to leave the room. Once Mother was safely downstairs and out of earshot, Luce followed the cat out from under the bed.

"Why did Father say I wasn't coming back? Do they think I've run away?" she asked the cat, realizing that she'd been out all night playing hide and seek.

The cat nudged Luce with its head and licked at her muddy toes. "Come with me. I want to show you something," he said.

Luce followed the cat down the stairs, through the back door to the narrow part in the bush in the far corner of the yard. She was feeling guilty about the mess and for getting Mother into trouble.

"I don't like it there at nighttime," Luce said. "I don't want to go back there and you can't make me."

"Luce . . ."

"I said no! And if I wanted to catch fleas, I'd go back to

school and sit next to Walter Flavelle. Just go away and leave me alone."

The cat turned angrily on the spot and disappeared onto the narrow path, leaving Luce standing alone and barefoot in the middle of the yard. She looked down at her feet—the motion caused the sun to set and the wind to rise—and the mud had all gone. She wiggled her toes but they were stiff, and for the first time since she'd awakened the night before, Luce realized she was rigid with cold.

With every step she took toward the house, an image flashed behind Luce's eyes: falling asleep, feverish under the afternoon sun; why Mother hadn't called her for supper; why Mother was always crying and Father was in a rotten mood.

Walter Flavelle had given her the ague and it killed her.

MOTHER WAS SITTING at the kitchen table with the *Warder* laid out flat on the table. Luce recalled Mother telling her once that there were only two ways to read the paper: with both hands, gripped firmly on either side, so you had a good handle on what you were reading, or with the paper laid out flat so you had both hands to support yourself if the news was that bad.

Luce stepped forward and read over her mother's shoulder.

PURDY'S MILLS STRUCK BY TRAGEDY
Eight more dead, all students of The Warder editor's
daughter, Miss Nelly Flood
Names of the Deceased:
Walter Flavelle
James Britton
Eleanor Cook
Mary Grant

John Meehan
Judith Baker
Matthew Aikins
Lucinda Walsh

Luce left Mother to support herself on the kitchen table and sat in the grass under the windowsill exactly as she had the night before. It was dark again and a black cat reappeared at the far corner of the yard.

"I don't need to come see that headstone. I know what it says." The cat climbed up on Luce's lap and let her scratch his ears and chin for a long time before he spoke. "I'm sorry for saying you had fleas. Walter Flavelle didn't have fleas either, did he?" The cat turned his head back and forth. "What happened?"

"The fever broke out on his skin. Walter was scratching at hives, not fleas."

"And me?"

"It was quick and painless. That's why you don't remember it."

"Are you here to take me back to the cemetery?"

"I'm not here for you this time, Luce," said the cat with a sad purr.

"What do you mean?"

The cat jumped off Luce's lap and onto the back step, pawing loudly at the door. It was Mother who answered.

"I'm awful sorry about the mud," said Luce, wrapping her arms tight around Mother's middle.

"Don't worry about the mud, darling." Mother smiled and held Luce out at arm's length so she could see her proper. "I knew it was you. I knew it."

"Is Father coming, too?" Luce asked hesitantly.

"Yes, Father's coming too. He'll join us when he's ready."

The cat meowed from across the yard, at the opening in the bush.

"Do you want to play with us?" said Luce, tugging at Mother's sleeve.

"Yes, darling. What shall we play?"

"Hide and seek. Come on, Cat has the best hiding spots."

***

Lori Rowsell—pronounced *Arousal* without the "*A*"—is a nurse by day, a mother always, and a writer whenever she can find a few precious minutes. She aims to deliver dark, gothic-themed stories, and is seeking an agent for her first young adult novel while polishing the second.

NORTHERN LIGHTS OVER NOGIE'S CREEK

Sara C. Walker

SLEEP WOULD NOT come, so I left my snoring boyfriend in the tent and went for fresh air. Down the cliffside, Nogie's Creek babbled playfully as it rushed from Bass Lake south to Sturgeon Lake, more of a small river than a creek. The night air was cooler than inside the tent, but the day's heat radiated out from the rock beneath the thin soil. I left our makeshift campsite under the cedar and birch trees and headed uphill for the clearing, hoping to catch more of that wind.

The property belonged to a friend of a friend of Brendan's— Curt, I think was his name—who said we could camp here. Brendan was thrilled at the fishing opportunities of the two lakes, while I was less than. Out in this wilderness there were no amenities, no people. The time with Brendan, just the two of us, was nice, but I was falling out of love with fishing and thinking of going home. I just didn't know how to break it Brendan.

As I was pondering shoe shopping in Bobcaygeon or antiquing in Fenelon Falls, I reached the clearing and stopped in my tracks. The sky was lit up with waving curtains of green, yellow, and pink. The Northern Lights. I knew about them, of course, but I'd never seen them before in my life.

"Don't be startled," someone called out.

My heart skipped a beat and came back rapid-fire. I searched wildly around me. Brendan was still sawing logs in the tent. Who was this person? Where was this person?

It was a male voice, but Brendan and I had been expecting to be alone out here. The sky was moonless—all the better for seeing the aurora, but not so good for eyeing up strange men in the night. I detected movement near the ground.

"I didn't think you noticed me," he said, "and I didn't want you be startled when you did."

"I'm pretty sure I would have jumped out of my skin either

way," I said. "We thought we had the property to ourselves. Are you Curt?"

"No, sorry. Name's Zane. Just passing through for the night."

"You must be another friend of Curt's, like Brendan, my boyfriend." I jerked a thumb in the direction of the tent. "Do you fish? We're here on a fishing trip."

"Can't say I've ever taken up fishing. I'm travelling. Thought I would take a moment to stop and watch the lights. You could too." He motioned at the ground beside him.

I wanted to—there was no knowing if I would ever have a chance to see the lights again—but staying meant being alone with this strange man. Just thinking about it that way was enough to freak me out, despite not feeling any sort of negative vibe from the man himself.

"Your choice," he added as he settled back to watch the light show.

What the hell, I decided. It wasn't like Brendan was far away. Besides, not every strange man was the next Paul Bernardo or Roch Thériault. Right?

I sat down beside him and lay back on the hard ground, squashing the wild daisies and dry grass. Just a few minutes and then I would head back to the tent.

The light danced and shimmered in the sky.

"Gosh, it's so nice," I said. "All that's missing is some classical music or something. I keep thinking I should hear those sky curtains rustling or feel the wind that moves them."

He made no more comment than a noncommittal grunt. *So much for pleasant conversation.*

"Where are you from?" I asked, but when he didn't reply I said, "I don't mean to pry or seem nosey; I just wanted to make conversation. We're from Toronto—well, Mississauga, really.

Perhaps you've been there? We've only been there a few years; I'm actually from Lindsay—you know, about a half-hour south of here?"

He shifted, and I got the impression my chatter was making him feel uncomfortable.

"I don't mean to be rude—"

"Nor do I," he said. "I just would rather listen to the lights."

"But there's nothing to hear," I blurted. I started to rethink this man. Perhaps he *was* mentally unstable after all. Perhaps I should think about calling it a night.

"The sound doesn't come from the light itself. You have to listen with your heart."

"You mean meditation," I said. "That stuff never worked for me. I tried to empty my mind of thoughts, but there's no stopping Niagara Falls, if you know what I mean."

"Try," he said. "Watch the light and listen to what your heart is telling you."

"All right," I said reluctantly.

I watched the light and listened to my heart, but all it was telling me was how useless this was, how I should go back to my sleeping bag because I would have to get into the boat and catch fish again tomorrow, how I was really not looking forward to yanking the poor creatures out of the water to judge their worthiness, how I really didn't want to go back to the city, either, to serving coffee and German pastries to endless streams of grumpy people, how the city didn't feel like home anymore, how I really needed to figure out what I wanted in life.

At some point I fell asleep. I woke with a start, my heart thudding in my chest. The questions tumbled in my mind: what happened, where was I, what was going on. The Northern Lights were still waving above me, mostly lime green and fading now, and the man—Zane—was still there. He drew in a slow, deep breath, as if he was holding back a frustrated sigh—the only acknowledgement of my falling asleep. I got the impression my being startled had disrupted his meditation.

I wondered what <u>his</u> heart was saying. I wondered if he'd only said those things to get me to shut up.

I stood up and brushed the dust from my shorts and t-shirt, intending to head back to the tent.

"How was it?" Zane asked.

"How was what?"

"The sound of the Lights."

"It—" I didn't know what to say. I'd heard nothing but my own worries, and I couldn't tell him that. Either I was doing something wrong or he was crazy. "It was fine. I guess. I just don't think it works for me."

He didn't say anything, and that was all the confirmation I needed.

I'd reached the edge of the clearing when he said, "See you again tomorrow night?"

My breath caught in my throat. Of all the things I was expecting him to say, that was not one of them. I'd had the distinct impression I was an intrusion, but perhaps that was not his thinking at all.

Before my mind could conjure all the reasons to say no, my mouth said yes. And before I could say anything more, my feet had the good sense to carry me back to the tent.

I SLEPT UNTIL midday. Brendan went fishing without me, which was just as well. I spent the afternoon wandering the area, making daisy chains, something I'd not done since I was child living in Lindsay. Back then I would leave suburbia for the fields, the nature trail, and the creek that edged the town limits.

By the time Brendan returned with a fresh catch for supper, I'd already made the fire and a pot of rice.

"I'm sorry I didn't go with you today," I started.

He shrugged a shoulder and continued to clean the fish. "You were dead to the world this morning, so I let you sleep."

"Yes, I—I couldn't sleep last night." I turned away and put butter in the cast iron pan. Telling Brendan about the lights meant telling him about Zane, and I didn't know how to explain any of it.

Brendan didn't seem to care about my sleeplessness, so I didn't bother trying to explain. He handed me the fillets and then popped the top of a can of beer he'd brought back from the river, where six-packs were tied to ropes and left in the water to stay cold.

I went back to the clearing that night after Brendan fell asleep. Zane and the Northern Lights were already there.

"I looked for you today," I said, "but didn't see any sign of you. Where do you keep yourself?"

"Around," he said, and nothing more. He lay with his fingers interlaced on his chest. It was hard to tell with him on the ground, but I had to guess he was about Brendan's height. Maybe shorter. With only the aurora to see by, I couldn't tell the exact shade of his hair, but it was dark; his complexion maybe olive, maybe tan—the aurora tinted everything green—but his features seemed friendly. He drew in a breath, as if gathering patience.

"I know, I know," I said. "It's time to listen."

I lay back against the rocky ground and stared up at the sky. My mind didn't go blank as it was supposed to. I kept wondering how I got here—not to Nogie's Creek, not exactly. How I got to living in the city, going on fishing trips on the weekends, serving coffee through the week. I didn't love any of that stuff. All those things were in my life because of Brendan. But who was this person I'd become? What happened to all the stuff I'd wanted to do with my life?

As happened the night before, I fell asleep, but this time I did not wake with a start. I knew exactly where I was before I opened my eyes. I drew in a breath of the cedar-infused air. The lights were fading. If Zane noticed I'd fallen asleep, he made no show of it.

"Zane? Can I ask you something?"

He grunted. I took that for a yes.

"What do you hear when you listen to the lights?"

"I hear what's in my heart," he said.

"And what's that?"

There was nothing but the song of crickets and the soft breeze soughing through the treetops for a few moments. Finally, he said, "I'm afraid I don't see how knowing the particulars of what's in my heart will help with what's in yours."

"It's just— I thought—" My cheeks burned with my embarrassment. I was a failure at meditation and I was failure at respecting other people's privacy.

"Your heart is your own," he said softly. "No one else can tell you what to feel."

That wasn't what I meant, but I didn't know how to explain myself.

"I wish I didn't have to return to the city. I wish I could see the aurora every night."

"So stay," he said.

"It's not that simple."

"It should be."

I concluded I was a disaster—at meditation, life in general, being a human being—and I returned to my tent. Zane didn't ask if I would be back.

Brendan fished alone again, but I was awake when he left. He chose to go without me—or I chose to stay, whichever. I didn't care enough to make a fuss. I made a daisy chain, but threw it in the river. The current didn't ask any questions; it just picked up the flowers and carried them away. There was something about that I needed to pay attention to, but for the moment it escaped me.

I returned to the clearing that night, but neither the lights nor Zane were there. I remembered he said he was just passing through, so I guessed he must have moved on.

The fishing trip came to an end. We packed up and went home.

SIX MONTHS LATER on a December morning, I was returning home from an early trip to the store. The sky was clear and sunny, the streets void of snow for once, having melted away in the night, and the city air was like a warm breath of spring.

I shifted the brown paper bag of groceries from one arm to the other as I reached into my pocket for the keys. Brendan had left for work hours ago, racing ahead to beat the traffic. So he'd said. The perfume clouding his shirts when he returned home late at night said something else.

I'd confronted him about it, but he brushed it off. I knew I needed to leave him, but I kept thinking I needed to stay to make it work. Leaving would mean giving up, wouldn't it? Besides, I had nowhere else to go, and there was no way I could afford to continue to live here on my coffee slinger's wage.

These past few months, the city had become a steady stream

of noise, traffic, and people around me, as if I was an immovable boulder. I often wondered what it would be like to happily float along with life, as they did. When had I last been happy? Was it when we were at Nogie's Creek? Or was it before then? Years ago?

I reached the door to the apartment and stopped to fish my keys out of my pocket. The toe of my shoe clunked against something on the mat. I shifted the loaded paper bag in my arms and turned to the side so I could have a look. It was a bright green pot with a burst of white daisies. The grocery bag fell from my arms and hit the floor of the hallway.

I searched the pot for some note, some card—something— but found only the florist's card sticking up on a plastic stick. I plucked it out. It was for the florist in Bobcaygeon.

As fast as my feet would carry me, I left the apartment, the fallen groceries, and everything else behind. I needed to rent a car.

THE FLORIST'S SHOP was in the street level of a Victorian building in "downtown" Bobcaygeon—the commerce section of the island village. The weather was unusually warm and sunny for December even this far north of the city; snowmelt darkened the sidewalk. Window boxes and urns outside the shop were brimming with boughs of evergreens and big bows of red satin ribbons. An elderly woman in an apron was there arranging the drooping branches, tightening the cheery bows.

"Nice day, isn't it?" she said when she saw me approach.

"I need to know who sent this," I blurted, and thrust the pot of daisies at her. The nearly three-hour drive from the city had taken its toll on my manners—or so I tried to tell myself.

Her smile never faltered. "Lovely, isn't it?"

"It came only with your card," I said.

"Did it? How unusual."

"What do you mean? Why is that unusual?"

She raised an eyebrow. "Because we don't carry pots of daisies."

I didn't understand. My body was alive with electricity and joy I'd not felt since those nights under the waving sky, but my mind was struggling.

"So you don't sell them? Then how did this show up at my apartment in Mississauga with your card in it?"

"To be quite sure, I don't know," she said. "We certainly don't deliver to Mississauga. Someone playing a practical joke, perhaps?"

My spine tingled. Did Brendan put the daisies on the doorstep? If so, why? Did he find out about the nights with Zane? From who? I'd not told him. Did he get up in the night and see the two of us there?

The flower seller noticed my distress, and seemed to take pity on me. "We could go inside and I could look at my records."

We did, and as expected, we discovered she had no record of deliveries to my apartment. She surmised someone had mistakenly attached one of her cards and had the flowers delivered from somewhere else, though why someone would do that was anyone's guess.

Crestfallen, I thanked her for her time and headed for the door. I'd come all this way, rented the car with my maxed-out credit card, paid for the gas with the last of my cash. But what else had I been expecting? Did I really believe I would find Zane here? Even if I did, what did that mean? We'd only spent a few nights under the stars together, barely said anything to each other. Coming here was ridiculously impulsive and stupid.

A red and black sign in the window caught my eye. *Help Wanted*, it said. I turned back to the woman.

"You're hiring?" I exclaimed.

She turned away from the plants she was watering. "I just put up that sign this morning," she said. "My employee won the lottery yesterday and is halfway to Fiji by now with her fiancé, and I'd like to retire soon." She smiled. "If only Fortuna would be so kind."

Her words felt like a dream, but the flower shop, with all its earthly smells, tasted real.

"Are you looking for work?" she asked.

My mouth worked before my mind kicked in. "As a matter of fact . . ."

We settled on terms of my employment. My first duty was to remove the sign from the window.

"I think this will work out quite well," she said, beaming. "The last girl lived in the apartment upstairs. You don't by chance happen to know anyone looking for a place, do you?"

My joy could hardly be contained. A smile pulled at my lips.

"As a matter of fact, I do."

I SETTLED INTO life at the flower shop easily. Turned out I had a knack for arranging flowers in ways other than knotting them into chains by their stems. Brendan didn't say much when I returned to gather my things from our apartment. If anything, he seemed relieved. I supposed part of me wanted him to beg me to stay; I was surprised to find myself relieved when he did not.

Though I stayed at the shop both day and night, months went by without me seeing any sign of Zane. So how exactly that card and pot of flowers came to me on exactly the right day, I might never know. I chalked it up to coincidence. Happenstance.

On my days off, I went hiking along Nogie's Creek, a mere five minutes' drive from my new home. But never saw sign of Zane there, either.

Before I knew it, summer was nearly upon us.

"Any plans for the long weekend?" my employer, June, asked. "This might be your last chance for a real vacation."

June planned to retire this summer, but intended to still keep tabs on the place, leaving me to mostly run things by myself. One of my first duties in that capacity would be to hire an assistant.

"Nope," I said. I'd thought of no more than sleeping late and catching up with the unfinished books on my nightstand. I'd started filling in a diary and making notes about a novel. I'd always wanted to be a writer.

She clucked her tongue. "Shame. I hear there's a solar flare happening this weekend. You should get out and take advantage of the sunny, hot weather we'll be having."

I shrugged. Sunny and hot didn't interest me.

"Oh, and I hear there's a good chance of viewing the Northern Lights, too," she said.

I froze. Time slowed between heartbeats. "Really?

"You don't keep track of the flares? You should. Nothing will dry out the plants faster than a burst of solar radiation." Her eyes narrowed in thought. "As a matter of fact, I believe there was a small one the day I hired you . . ."

I could hardly hear her over the slamming of my heart in my chest and the blood rushing in my ears.

"Are you feeling all right, dear? You look a bit pale. Why don't you start your weekend right now?"

"Oh, no. I . . ." But I didn't know which question I was answering.

"Go on. I'll lock up the shop." She took me by the shoulders and directed me out to the backroom to the stairs leading to my apartment. I climbed the stairs, insisting I was all right, just tired. She returned to the shop after I promised to call if I needed anything.

I sat on the floor of my living room, thinking about solar flares, auroras, and the contents of my heart. Did solar flares cause auroras? I didn't know, but worse, I knew even less about what was in my own heart.

Did I want to go to Nogie's Creek again seeking Zane? Of course I did. But why? Curiosity more than anything, I supposed. I wanted to know how he felt about me, but admitting that made me feel like no a child on the school playground.

To be honest, the question of his liking me wasn't at the top of my list. If he didn't like me, he wouldn't have invited me to return to the clearing. In truth, I wanted to spend time with him again. I'd learned from him and I felt like I had so much more to learn. And although I'd felt completely uncomfortable in my own skin under those lights, I'd also never felt closer to my own true self. Being with Brendan, I went along doing all the things he wanted to—watching hockey, going fishing, visiting his friends. None of those things were me. But watching the Northern Lights . . . that was for me. Brendan would never understand that, while Zane already did.

The light from the window slid across the floor as I sat there debating what to do with myself. There were far worse problems in the world, and here I was fretting over a boy liking me or not. I felt like a fool. I was going to miss my opportunity to see the lights again if I didn't pull myself together. I got up off the floor, changed into jeans and hiking boots, and set out for Nogie's Creek.

BY THE TIME I set out on the trail through Curt's property, the world had shifted into that in-between time. With the sun below the horizon, it was almost as though someone had hit the pause button on the wind and the soft blue sky. Birds chirped from high in the trees. The forest floor was either rock and moss and tree roots or hollows built up with layers of fallen leaves and needles. Darkness rose from the shadows on the ground, filling in the blanks between the trees. By the time I reached the clearing—our clearing?—full dusk had transformed the sky as if someone had spilled a bottle of indigo ink. I lay down among the young meadow daisies and waited.

This would make a good story, I thought. This woman, chasing after a man who was no more than dream. Would she catch him?

Did Zane even exist outside my imagination? Who was he without all the characteristics I'd projected onto him? Who was he really?

I didn't notice if the man or the lights arrived first. If pressed, I would have to say they arrived at the same time.

"I wasn't sure you'd come," he said.

"Funny, I was about to say the same thing," I replied.

There was so much I wanted to know—who he was, where he went, what he liked to do besides travel—but I didn't have the heart to ask. I supposed I would always have trouble with invading people's privacy that way.

"I read that the aurora is considered by some to be a celestial wedding." My cheeks went hot. Of all the myths I'd read, why did I mention that one?

"It's not," he said.

We fell silent again as I clamped down on my foolish tongue.

After a while, as I started to drift asleep, he said, "It's a bridge."

I smiled sleepily. "So the Vikings were right. The lights lead the fallen warriors to Valhalla."

"No," he said. "The lights are a bridge from my home to yours."

As I slid off the edge of consciousness into sleep, I wondered what he meant by that. The lights were fading, but I hadn't yet thanked him for the pot of daisies. I hadn't yet told him about my new place or my job or relationship status.

"Zane . . ." I reached my hand over to where he was lying next to me on the grass, but found only empty air. He was gone.

Was he telling the truth about being from another world? Or was he nothing more than a construct of my imagination? I supposed in the end, it didn't matter who he was, where he went, what he liked to do, or even if he liked me. He'd shown me the way back to myself, back to Kawartha Lakes, to the place where my heart belonged.

***

Sara C. Walker is a Canadian author with published urban fantasy novels for teens, action romance novels for adults, and short stories of every variety. She also works at a library, where she takes particular pride in getting readers addicted to new stories. Sara lives and writes next to a lake in the beautiful cottage country of Central Ontario with her husband, three sons, two cats, and one dog. Her short story, "If Wishes Were Pennies," was a semifinalist for the John Kenneth Galbraith Literary Award.

Manufactured by Amazon.ca
Bolton, ON

16786998R00079